APRIL MOORE

GIFTS

AND
CALLINGS

DEEPER FOUNDATIONS:
WHAT CAN YOU DO WITH THE FIRE OF THE HOLY SPIRIT LIVING INSIDE YOU?

-EXPANDED EDITION-

Gifts and Callings

DEEPER FOUNDATIONS: WHAT CAN YOU DO WITH THE FIRE OF THE HOLY SPIRIT LIVING INSIDE YOU?

2ND EDITION

April Moore

Publisher: April Moore

Houston, TX

Expanded 2nd Edition

Copyright© 1st Edition 2016 and 2019 Expanded 2nd Edition by April Moore

All rights reserved. No part of this publication may be reproduced, distributed or transmitted in any form or by any means, including photocopying, recording, or other electronic or mechanical methods, without the prior written permission of the publisher, except in the case of brief quotations embodied in critical reviews and certain other noncommercial uses permitted by copyright law. For permission requests, write to the publisher, addressed "Attention: Permissions Coordinator," at the email address below.

Author: April Moore/ Publisher: April Moore

KEMinistries@Gmail.com

KEMinistries.com

Copyright Notices:

All Scripture quotations, unless otherwise indicated, are taken from the Holy Bible, New King James Version. Scripture taken from the New King James Version®. Copyright © 1982 by Thomas Nelson. Used by permission. All rights reserved.

Scripture quotations marked (AMPCE) are taken from the Amplified Bible, Copyright © 1954, 1958, 1962, 1964, 1965, 1987 by The Lockman Foundation. Used by permission.

Ordering Information:

Quantity sales. Special discounts are available on quantity purchases by corporations, associations, and others. For details, contact the "Special Sales Department" at the email address above.

Gifts and Callings, Deeper Foundations: What Can You Do With The Fire of the Holy Spirit Living Inside You? / April Moore. Expanded 2nd Edition.

ISBN Print: 978-0-9984826-3-7 and 978-0-9984826-4-4

Hardback: 978-0-9984826-5-1

★★ 5 Star Reviews! ★★

This book is more than good, it is life changing...

Reading the contents of this book, has changed my life. She has put language to what God is doing in churches, in ministry, in the Kingdom. We are finding identity in Christ, deeper relationship, and language for who we are in the spirit. You understand more than your gifts, it begins to unlock your purpose and releases limitations. I have heard the Author teach and it is even richer. You must read this and bring her to train your groups!

- Eva Paulino, Reviewer

This is a must read for churches today!

This book is a powerful tool and very much needed in the body of Christ! It answered a lot of questions that I had concerning gifts and callings and brought clarity to each function. It's very easy to read and understand. I will definitely recommend this book to everyone I know!

- Colleen Campa, Amazon Reviewer

This book makes lofty concepts very practical and easy to understand...

We are no doubt in the Information Age, however amidst all of the information floating around all over the place, I still found myself ignorant to the inner workings of the gifts and callings God bestowed on His people. THIS BOOK makes lofty concepts very practical and easy to understand! It is filled with sound, biblical revelation! It is so valuable and needed for individuals, local ministries and the body of Christ as a whole! We need to be equipped in order to equip them and help them tap into their Gifts and Callings!

- Amazon Reviewer

Excellent...

I have been telling my friends about this book. I read chapter one and started two. I am mind blown April Moore made this so plain yet engaging. I know that this book will help me walk heavy in my gifts.

- Aisha Nauling, Amazon Reviewer

A Great Book...

I had many questions and the writer answered them. The writing was easy enough to understand. It was like I was drinking every Word. There is life in every point made. There is a personal activation in reading these pages. Thank you!

- D. B., Amazon Reviewer

I recommend that all Pastors and Teachers get this book and ...

The quality and content of this book is fabulous. As a teacher in the body of Christ, this is the type of scriptural based content that is needed in order to teach this spiritual concept. I recommend that all Pastors and Teachers get this book and do a study on this very important subject. You are anointed to teach and bring the fire out in those you touch.

- Meme Spearman, Author and Amazon Reviewer

Excellent Book...

What an amazing book! Easy to read, packed with information that leaves you desiring to learn more. A must read for everyone.

- Aisha Shepard, Amazon Reviewer

Table of Contents

Chapter 1 – Big Kingdom Picture 19
- *Why is This Book Important?* 21
- *The Back Story on Gifts* 23
- *First Things First* 25
- *How to Use This Training* 27
- *Journal Questions:* 28

Chapter 2 – Language and Operation 29
- *What are gifts and how do we get them?* 30
- *How do you receive gifts?* 32
- *Laying on of Hands and Prayer* 33
- OTHER IMPORTANT LANGUAGE 35

Chapter 3 – Gifts of the Holy Spirit 40
- REVELATION GIFTS 40
  - *Discerning of Spirits* 42
  - *Word of Knowledge* 49
  - *Word of Wisdom* 52
  - *Dream Interpretation* 53
  - *Journal Questions:* 55
- INSPIRATIONAL GIFTS 56
  - *Tongues* 57
  - *Interpretation of Tongues* 59
  - *Prophecy* 61
  - *Prophetic Guidelines* 64
  - *Journal Questions:* 66
- POWER GIFTS 67
  - *Faith* 68
  - *Healings* 72
  - *Working of Miracles* 73
  - *Things to Remember* 76
  - *Journal Questions:* 78

Chapter 4 - The Design Gifts 79
- *Administration* 83
- *Leadership* 84
- *Exhortation* 85
- *Teaching* 86
- *Mercy* 88
- *Giving* 90

Helps/Service	*91*
Journal Questions:	*94*
Chapter 5 – Callings	**95**
Terminology	*97*
How do you know you are called?	*97*
Gift-Level Anointing vs Calling	*99*
The Process	*102*
Ascension Gifts	*107*
APOSTLES	108
PROPHETS	111
TEACHERS	117
PASTORS	120
EVANGELISTS	125
Ascension Gift Key	*129*
Journal Questions:	*131*
YOUR CHARGE	131
Prayer of Activation	*132*
Appendix - Bishops, Elders and Deacons	**133**
Bishops	*134*
Elders	*134*
Deacons	*135*
SUGGESTED READING	139
REFERENCES USED	140
ABOUT THE AUTHOR	141

DEDICATION:

I want to thank God first for truly being good to me and giving me the most important gifts of all, my salvation and my family.

To Morris Moore, my husband, thank you for encouraging me and believing in our dream. You are righteous, honorable and full of integrity and you are mine. Soon the world will know what a true man of honor you are. There is a part of Christ in you that sets the standard and I love you completely, my handsome sweetheart.

To my daughters:

Taylor, my first born, you are so courageous. Your path will one day be as clear as the noon day sun, and you will blaze the trail that you were born to blaze. To whom much is given, much is required. I bless you and love you so much honey.

Brityn, you are full of joy that bubbles over. This joy and laughter are what will keep you strong. You embrace wisdom and righteousness and will be great in the Kingdom. Your task is heavy at times, but you will lean on your training to rise above and conquer mountains. Be meek but bold my sweet baby. Mommy loves you so dearly.

My spiritual daughter, Eva Paulino, no one compares to you in His eyes. You will carry the gospel with grace, passion and love. This will make you a force to be reckoned with. Wilkins and the kids are your foundation and your rock. Son, love her well because you are mighty and full of everything that she is on the inside, but you manifest it with courage, strength and authority. Wilkins, you are the best! May you both always be ONE in Him!

I speak peace, wisdom and life to you all...joy, love, purity and prosperity. May you always overcome, daughters! You all in your way bring me great joy. I am proud of you individually for who you are and who I see you becoming. I believe in you.

To everyone reading this, I declare that your legacy is rich and that you will know the hope of His calling for you and the richness of your inheritance.

ACKNOWLEDGMENTS

I want to thank my Mom, Verna Thomas because without you, I wouldn't be here (wink). You taught me how to be a lady and introduced me to Christ. You have always been there. I love you, thank you and appreciate you!

Dad, we love you and we are always here for you. Thank you for always believing in me!

To Meme Spearman with www.LadyMBooks.com*, thank you for the direction and the fabulous book cover. You help bring dreams to life!*

Thank you, Lenita Davis, founder of Right Words Editing, for your editing expertise and for being a great friend. Your friendship has been refreshing and invaluable to us. Thank you again for EVERYTHING.

The people that love and stand with you make up part of who you are. I wanted to honor everyone. So, to everyone I may have missed that was there to encourage and believe in us, thank you!

"What is in the pencil is greater than what is around it. The [gifts] in you are greater than the environment surrounding you. Your potentials will change your environment."
— Israelmore Ayivor

"A wonderful gift may not be wrapped as you expect."
— Jonathan Lockwood Huie

Chapter 1 – Big Kingdom Picture

Prophetically speaking, we are in a time where the world has grown colder, the people of God are rapidly becoming lukewarm and ill-equipped to deal with the state of the Kingdom of God. Many of us see that change is needed and people are hurting, but we don't always know how to help. Also, many of us have seen the gifts in operation, some by great people of God and some by imposters, and it is sometimes hard to discern which voices to listen to. Therefore, the next few statements I will make are perhaps *just* as important as the whole of the book you are now holding in your hands. The Kingdom of God needs people who are equipped to deal with the times we are in. We need to allow the Kingdom of God to be revealed in our lives so that we can be supernatural change agents in this earth realm. We know that our Christ lovingly died to bring us salvation from our sins and He rescued us from eternal separation from God, but His victorious blood was shed for so much more! We have also been restored to our rightful place in the Kingdom of God because of the death, burial, resurrection *and ascension* of Jesus Christ, our Lord and Savior. The world *needs* us to truly bring the light and power of God to them so that their hearts may be turned back to Him. People need to know that the greatest power existing belongs to God. The world is hurting and needs the refreshing that comes through salvation and grace from the Father. Soldiers in the Kingdom that are ill need the restoration that the gifts God gives to us can bring. Faith needs to be restored to the Kingdom so we can come to the realization of our purpose amid the mundane shifting of life. People of God need deliverance and freedom from bondage.

    We have believed the lies of the enemy for so long that we fail to be true believers of God. What do I mean? I am not talking about the faith that saved you. In that, many of us have done well. I mean the faith that helps us to believe the *whole* Bible and the *whole* Word that God brings to us so that we can continue to advance the Kingdom. Lies will say, "Yes God can heal, but probably not me." Or, "Prophecy and all of that was only for Biblical times to lay the foundation of the church." Or, commonly we hear, "We live, and we die, and that is all there is to life." These are all lies. Christ shed His precious blood to make us victorious like Him! You are more than just a cog in some wheel of life. You were born to make an impact. And, there is no Biblical support that shows all those things mentioned above are done away with. It did help to establish the church, but it is needed to *continue* building the Kingdom. We plainly see that there is much division just within Christianity alone. We also see that this world is increasingly becoming darker.

Yes, there is a big picture here and you fit right in it. Despite how you may feel at times, you are world reformers and Kingdom shakers. Your life, along with all you've already overcome, proves that with God you *are* more than a conqueror because you have defeated the enemy repeatedly with each breath that you take. You are still here, and your story is not over. In a way, God has given us the ability to become super heroes in our own rights through the gifts He gave us – right where we are in the areas of our lives that we thought were mundane and routine. He has called us to a life filled with His supernatural power. You have purpose, you have destiny and there is more to this life than what you see with mere eyes. No one is too young and certainly not too old, so as long as you have breath in your body, I charge you to *run this race and finish strong*. The giftings that we will discuss will be *your* game changer!

Why is This Book Important?

So, the book you now hold is a key to unlock the light of God and to change the atmosphere around you in your homes, your professions, your church and your areas of influence. It can help build a foundation in your life so that you truly cause tremendous change and are not defeated. The objective of creating this training is to provide a strong Biblical background while learning about the gifts of the Spirit. Revelatory teaching is wonderful and viable when truly

April Moore

lead by the Spirit of God, but a strong Biblical foundation diminishes error and misuse of scriptural gift operations. It is true that there are many ways in which the Holy Spirit operates and that it could not all be written in the Bible. John said as much in John 21:25, which states, "And there are also many other things that Jesus did, which if they were written one by one, I suppose that even the world itself could not contain the books that would be written. Amen." So, while we want to have strong Biblical foundation, we do not want to negate or diminish the power of God in the many ways He reveals the giftings through different manifestations and works in our lives. So, in this training, you will see both teaching methods present, but the emphasis is to help you see the giftings in operation in the Word of God.

There is so much to be shared concerning the Kingdom of God, prophetic expression, the realm of the spirit and the gifts given by God to us. It cannot all be covered here, so this book majors on deepening the foundation of some of these subjects. It serves as a comprehensive Biblical foundation that focuses on the gifts of the Spirit and gives fundamental understanding to the callings of God.

Training from this material has also been of great use to those who have been walking in their giftings and callings for many years because it provides further clarification – it gives a broader foundation of the gifts and different ways they manifest. So, if you have already been operating, and not completely new to this, it can greatly enrich your experience and give a better frame of reference. Subsequently, God can use *you* greater or in different ways.

Furthermore, if you are looking for resources, deeper training and activation, Kingdom Enlightenment Ministries can help. We offer training for core leaders and teams through various means, so that they are equipped to lead this training in your area or congregation. Find more, go to KEMinistries.com.

The Back Story on Gifts

In the Garden of Eden, man had perfect communion with God. The spirit and natural realm co-existed so that one had access to both realms. However, after the fall of man, there was a separation from God that only He could redeem. Gifts are a beautiful part of God's plan to redeem the earth and brings parts of heaven to earth for God's glory. It is a gift that He allows us access to the spirit realm, and it is part of God's grace.

Grace is **charis (khar'ece)** in Greek, the original language of the New Testament. It means God's good will toward us, His kindness, beneficial favor and gift. So, you can almost use gift and grace interchangeably. His grace is a bounty. Webster defines this type of bounty as meaning something given or occurring in generous amounts. God is liberally giving His gifts to man as one way to redeem the earth and merge the realm of the spirit and the earth together in various ways through His people. We have been given authority here on earth, so when we open ourselves up to the use of the gifts we are given, we are saying "Yes Lord! Come into the earth, I give it back to you so your glory can be deposited here."

April Moore

Why Gifts?

Gifts, in essence, are like getting glimpses of Jesus Himself in others. Some will have many gifts and may flow differently during different times of their lives, while others may have a measure of a gift that doesn't operate as boldly or on a regular basis. Either way, the gifts we see in others are there to mature, empower and show us what we can do, what we should do, or how to help to serve those around us. Therefore, gift assessments are so important. They not only should tell you what gift you have, but also how strong it's being expressed in your life. Seeing how weak or strong a gift is may inspire you to strengthen those that are dormant within you.

Gifts enable you to manifest certain activities in the spirit realm. The gift is like a radio station that you are tuned into and if it is submitted to God, it can be very useful to the Body of Christ and for winning or restoring souls to Christ. However, some do not submit their gifts to God, so the signal is either tainted by or completely taken over by the demonic kingdom. In other cases, it is simply a lack of maturing in what God has gifted them with. When the former is true, it can appear to be very real, but it is merely information that the enemy has observed and is relaying through the "station" from *his* network.

However, some do not submit their gifts to God, so the signal is either tainted by or completely taken over by the demonic kingdom. In other cases, it is simply a lack of maturing in what God has gifted them with. When the former is true, it can appear to be very real, but it is merely information that the enemy has observed and is relaying through the "station" from *his* network.

The enemy may also be using people in some gifts for his own purposes and agendas. For example, psychics, mediums, fortune tellers, and false prophets all utilize this demonic network through familiar spirits and demons of different kinds. Read Leviticus 19:31, Leviticus 20:6-7, and Acts 16:16-18 for God's heart on this matter. There is more on this that we are unable to cover at this time, but heed to the following: *All of these gifts and callings can be counterfeited by the enemy or out of your own soulish understanding, but the explanations here show the gifts in operation under the directive of the Holy Spirit so you will know the difference.*

First Things First

In 1 Corinthians 13:1-7, it is explained to us how important love is, and while it describes other fruit, it focuses on love. Many believers esteem the gifts God gives above the love of God. But this scripture shows that if love is not present then the gifts mean absolutely nothing. This is being spoken right in the middle of Paul teaching more in depth about many of the gifts. So, it is not saying that gifts are not important, it is simply saying that the fruit of love takes precedence over giftings. Galatians 5:16 explains that if you walk in the spirit you will not fulfil the lust of the flesh, and then explains how to do that through the fruit of the Spirit.

April Moore

But the fruit of the Spirit is love, joy, peace, longsuffering, kindness, goodness, faithfulness, gentleness, self-control. Against such there is no law. And those who are Christ's have crucified the flesh with its passions and desires. If we live in the Spirit, let us also walk in the Spirit. (Galatians 5:22-25)

Galatians Chapter 5 is saying to decrease operating in the flesh so that we can operate in purity of character. We must produce the fruit of the Spirit! The manifestation of the fruit is what determines if we are walking in the Spirit versus walking in the flesh. But even in that, the lack of fruit does not necessarily prevent one from operating in spiritual gifts. In other words, even a Christian who is not yet mature, or who is carnal in actions, may still operate in spiritual gifts. Carnality is something that we should grow from as Christians as we become more Holy Spirit lead. It is a never-ending process as we behold the Lord and become more like Him and yield to his ways. This process is what begins to eradicate carnality in our lives. We *will always* be working on our growth, which makes these gifts *truly* a gift. It should be something that produces humility in our hearts.

It is important to clarify another scripture before we proceed. Romans 11:29 KJV says, "For the gifts and calling of God are without repentance." The NKJV states, "For the gifts and the calling of God *are* irrevocable." This is *not* referring to God allowing the operation of gifts in people and then not taking the gift away when they fall into sin. It is also not allowing people to behave in whatever manner they choose. The common line you will hear is, "Well God does give gifts without repentance." This scripture is referring to the gifts of grace and righteousness. In context, it is the grace we receive from salvation in Christ, righteousness, and the call to relationship with Him. This knowledge is the foundation of our faith and should provoke us to continue growing in Him and into the likeness of Christ. The way to do that is to learn the Word of God and to develop the fruit of the Spirit. The fruit isn't something you just possess, it is something that you *activate* and use as you relate to those around you.

How to Use This Training

This training is primarily geared toward being used in a group setting where a teacher is leading a group through the various chapters. You will find that group training provides a rich and powerful platform to not only learn but develop and activate spiritual giftings. However, in the absence of such support, you can carefully study this training and use it as a deep study on the topics presented for personal training. While reading, you may see the Greek word for each gift, and if needed, the English definition to give a more complete meaning.

April Moore

Journal Questions:

1. What are some of your fears when it comes to operating in your spiritual gifts?

2. What would your life look like if you were to be more open to operating in spiritual gifts?

3. Do you have certain people groups that you would find it hard to love and minister to? (Example: Those who have committed certain crimes or live lifestyles in which you don't approve).

4. What are some of the questions you have regarding spiritual gifts?

5. Go to www.KEMinistries.com to take your Spiritual Gift Assessment.

CHAPTER 2

Chapter 2 – Language and Operation

We often hear terms being used among Christians, but some of us are unaware of what they mean when it comes to spiritual gifts. Overall, this makes the operation of gifts seem very mysterious. As I have trained and activated believers in giftings over the years, I realize there are other areas that needed to be explained in our book and not just in training settings. Language is very important. It builds your vocabulary and frames the world around you. So, I wanted to help you understand some of the language and basics of gift operation. I also want to stretch your understanding of some of these things.

Can I have more than one gift?

It is true that God distributes gifts to us according to his will, according to 1 Corinthians 12:11, but many take these verses to mean that you can only have one gift. This is error. God can give you as many or as few spiritual gifts as is needed. The list in 1 Corinthians 12 was just given to explain *how* God distributes gifts to each of us, and not to be taken literally that He only gives one gift to each person. It is also good to note the sovereignty of God that is shown in that scripture. He is the one that wills to give gifts to us, but also know that you can ask. Even though there is liberty in being children of God, it should be mentioned that access to the spirit realm without the authorization or the leading and moving of the Lord opens you to dark or demonic realms. There is a section of gifts (termed Design Gifts, which relate more to your natural makeup) that we will talk about that does not require this supernatural access in the same way that other gifts do.

So, we will cover what gifts really are, how gifts are given by God, and how they operate in the spirit realm. We will also talk about how gifts are transferred, imparted and activated.

What are gifts and how do we get them?

The Kingdom of God is His people, and He pours into our spirits and builds us from the inside out. All of these gifts are attributes and functions of Him that He is giving us access to. Think of them as pieces of Him that He gives us to build His kingdom here on earth, and we use them in building people and possessing territory.

After writing the first edition of this book, the Lord began to reveal much more to me regarding spiritual gifts and how they operate. We often view them as though they are these little things that God put in a box and placed inside of us, and then we can open that box by the leading of the Holy Spirit and get pieces of the contents. Then, when it's over, we close the box. This is not exactly how it works. I will build on this subject so that the whole of how they work and operate can be easily grasped.

Something very important to remember is that gifts are more like keys…not boxes. God gives these keys to access certain places or realms in the spirit so that He can work through us in the earth. He has given us authority here on earth, but it is up to us to *open the door* so that, through Him, Heaven can pour through.

How does it work?

I want you to understand how this works. However, after reading the next few chapters, you may need to return to this section, having gained greater understanding.

So, we established that gifts are more like keys that give you access. God sovereignly gives you the authority by authorizing you to open gates to areas, or we will say, realms of the spirit. Our bodies give us access to the natural realm, but our own spirits give us access to the spirit realm. Our born-again spirits have the same 5 senses that our natural body does (we will cover this more in Discernment in Chapter 3). Your natural body is an interface or door to the natural realm (earth), and your spirit is a door to the spirit realm. The gift is a *key* to an area of the spirit realm and that area is where the gift resides. *It is a gift because you have been granted special access to the spirit realm*. Some examples are the gift realm of prophecy or the gift realm of faith. Each realm of the spirit has a gate, door, or portal. Any of those words would be accurate. Your spiritual authorization gives you the key to open the gate of certain gift realms. So, if you have a gift of healing, you have been authorized by God to open that realm so that it flows through you. You then receive it in your spirit and pour it out to the natural world.

How do you receive gifts?

In short, God is sovereign, and He gives us access to the gift realms. It starts with Him. Some gifts are easy for you to access on demand while there are others God may cause to come through you at different times. In either case, you *can* ask God for gifts. You can also ask God to increase how your gifts operate. Knowing *what the gifts are* is a big part of gaining more access. This is because many times people find that they have been operating in gifts unaware because they didn't know what that gift realm was! So, the fuller your understanding, the fuller the operation. Just like with an electronic device or a vehicle, the more you understand, the better and more *accurately* you can operate. Furthermore, just like vehicles, there are avenues through which we receive gifts.

Natural Family

Many times, you will see gifts access travel through family bloodlines. This goes for all categories of gifts that are taught in this book. You may notice on one side of your family, many people seem to have a lot of dreams or visions, or many of them teach in school settings. Or, on the other side of your family, you may have people that are strong exhorters, or who have great administration or leadership gifts. Because God established His kingdom model on the earth through families first, it is not far-fetched that there are Kingdom assignments and functions that God purposes in families. A great Biblical example of this is 2 Timothy 1:5. Paul mentions to Timothy that faith was in his grandmother, his mother, and Paul believed it was also operating in Timothy's life.

Spiritual Family or Connected Groups

There are also times when gifts begin to fall on groups of people. We see that on the day of Pentecost when tongues of fire rested on the whole group (Acts 2:1-4) and when King Saul and others from his troop were found prophesying among the prophets (1 Samuel 19).

Laying on of Hands and Prayer

In 2 Timothy 1:6, Paul spoke about stirring up a gift within Timothy through the laying on of hands. Also, in James 5:14, James is saying that if there are any that are sick, the elders can be called to pray over them. This suggests that prayer can open the healing realm too.

A Close, More Intimate Walk with God

Note that it isn't just elders or ministers who can pray over you for breakthrough. Many times, they do carry heavier authority, but *you* can also pray for others and even yourself. This authority to open realms is not exclusive nor restrictive, and can come from a closer connection and relationship with God. Yes, it is a gift and many believers, despite maturity level or title, can operate in gifts. It is the delight of the Lord to see those in communion with Him occupy their spiritual places of expression.

Intimacy is about transforming and becoming more Christlike as a result of His presence, rather than being set on a journey just *to get.* In realization of the state of our hearts as well as that of humanity, we draw closer to Him in faith for comfort, answers and reassurance. This is not only because He is the Gift Giver but because He is the Father who first loved us before we ever knew we were known.

Other Important Language

What is the anointing?

Operating in a gift is operating in an anointing. The word anointing in the Bible is **Chrio (Khree'-o)** in Greek. It means to smear oil on for service in some capacity. This word is used in many different ways, but let's stay close to how it relates to spiritual gifts. Anointing with oil in the natural is a point of contact in receiving something spiritual from God. This would be an outward expression of the anointing. Or, spiritually we see the anointing as an attribute of God being smeared onto our spiritual being for some act of service. So, when someone says you are anointed, they are saying that you are smeared with a supernatural ability from God. It doesn't have to just pertain to spiritual gifts. It can be used in reference to God smearing, like oil, a supernatural ability onto a natural ability. Singing, playing an instrument, athletic abilities, or even the way you do your job are just some of the areas in which God can anoint you for. It means that God's hand is on you, giving you more power than you could have exhibited from yourself. So yes, all glory goes to God in everything that we do. When we yield even our natural talents and abilities and allow God to breathe on it, we are allowing Him to anoint and empower us!

April Moore

What is Impartation and Transference?

These two words are essentially the same in function, so we will use them interchangeably. When you give to others power or virtue from your gift, you do not lose what was transferred. Impartation is how the Kingdom of God is built! This is what multiplies, builds and strengthens people. You are transferring power from the spirit realm to others.

One way you transfer this spiritual power is through words. Words are extremely powerful, particularly when we receive them. So revelatory words like a *word of knowledge*, *word of wisdom*, and even inspirational words like *prophetic words* pack the power of faith to shift people's lives. We will go more in depth later, but faith opens a supernatural highway to receive anything in the spirit and anchors it here in the natural realm until what you are believing for manifests. So, when faith is in operation, it opens the pathway for the words to manifest and take shape in the physical realm.

Another way that gifts can transfer is through contact. Either touching or being near an object can activate transfer. We can pray over anointing oil, cloths, or other objects for transfer to people. Even Peter's shadow activated a transfer of anointing from him, and others were healed (Acts 5:15).

Activation

As we said, the gift is a key, or authorized access, into a specific realm in the spirit. But *activation* of the gift itself is power from God being released into the earth. This gives clarified meaning to The Lord's Prayer when Jesus says, "Your Kingdom come, your will be done, on earth as it is in Heaven" (Matthew 6:10). God gives gifts so that what resides in Heaven can flood the earth realm.

In 2 Timothy 1:6, when Paul mentioned stirring up the gift of God that was already in Timothy by laying hands on Him, contact with Him also helped to *activate* that dormant gift.

Your mouth can even activate a gift. If someone experiences trouble with speaking in tongues, they may need to begin uttering sounds until the Holy Spirit "jump starts" the flow. Also, at times I have the unction to deliver a prophetic word to a person while having only little information from the Lord. He will prompt me to move in faith, with the few words I have, and by the time I open my mouth more revelation comes. Often, it can turn out that I have massive "downloads" for a person, taking several minutes or more to deliver, but I would never have known what God had in store without speaking up in faith first. The activation of speaking opens up revelation.

There are thousands of ways to self-activate and activate others in their gifts. Educating people helps to activate things that may be dormant, which is why this book is so important. There are also activation exercises that can be done for some of the gifts.

April Moore

Laying hands and imparting a gift, as we just saw can activate the gift. Also, speaking to the gift in someone under prophetic utterance can activate and bring forth their gift. There is a great book on gift activations by John Eckhardt called "Prophetic Activation: Break Your Limitation to Release Your Prophetic Influence". It specifically helps to activate different realms in the spirit and more.

My favorite is the blindfold activation. It is something that I do often. This is where you blindfold a person or group of people, and then you place a person in front of them. You can play prophetic worship music while the blindfolded person focusses on their spiritual senses. It is best to have a coach go around and observe because they may have to help the participants. For example, ask them: "Do you hear anything? Words, music, phrases?" "Do you see anything like colors, pictures, or movies?" "Do you smell, taste, or feel something out of the ordinary?" If any of these are the case, they are likely discerning something in the spirit realm, and if they are new to this, they may even doubt what they are sensing. Have them share anyway to help them determine if it is a God direction. Typically, it won't make sense right away. Then, prompt them to ask God what it means or ask Him what He is saying. Sometimes people will be inexperienced, and they may need help from their coach. The coach does not need to be a prophet, just someone experienced in sensing things in the spirit and even interpreting visions and senses. Many times, the person needs to start speaking to get the rest of the information flowing.

If someone is experienced in flowing in the spirit in this way, I will double or even triple activate them. This means, I will keep them blindfolded and place a person in front of them. After they give a prophetic word to the first person, I will remove the first person they gave a word to and place another person in front of them. Then, I will possibly go through another cycle with a third person. This helps to stretch their gift. Different people bring different feelings, images, etc. Another thing to be aware of is spiritual focus issues. When a person is placed in front of another, they may have trouble focusing because they are picking up on other people standing nearby.

April Moore

CHAPTER 3

Chapter 3 – Gifts of the Holy Spirit

There are diversities of <u>gifts</u>, but the same Spirit. There are differences of <u>ministries</u>, but the same Lord. And there are diversities of <u>activities</u>, but it is the same God who works all in all. But the manifestation of the Spirit is given to each one <u>for the profit of all</u>: for to one is given **the word of wisdom** *through the Spirit, to another* **the word of knowledge** *through the same Spirit, to another* **faith** *by the same Spirit, to another* **gifts of healings** *by the same Spirit, to another the* **working of miracles**, *to another* **prophecy**, *to another* **discerning of spirits**, *to another* **different kinds of tongues**, *to another the* **interpretation of tongues**. *But one and the same Spirit works all these things, distributing to each one individually as He wills. (1 Corinthians 12:4-11)*

Revelation Gifts

The Revelation gifts are *discerning of spirits (discernment), word of knowledge* and *word of wisdom*. *Discerning of spirits* will reveal or show you things from God's vantage point through many different means that we will discuss. When you speak under the revelation of these gifts, you are speaking or describing the intellect, emotions and counsel of God. Even the nuances of impressions are interpreted, and bring life to what God is saying, in your own words. As you explain what God has revealed to you, it can be like describing the actual words or body language of one individual to another.

Some gifts are used interchangeably but have different functions, so clarity will be brought to those specifics. For example, with the *word of knowledge*, *word of wisdom* and *prophecy* (explained later in the book), one is often confused for the other. The following will give distinct characteristics that will help you to differentiate them.

April Moore

Discerning of Spirits

Diakrisis (dee-ak'-ree-sis)- distinguishing, discerning, or judging. It also means to separate one from another.

Discerning (Webster's)- Recognizing or identifying right from wrong, including motives. Also, to detect with your senses.

Spirit- Pneuma (pnyoo'-mah)- In the Bible, this word was used for the following and more: God, Christ's Spirit, angels, demons, human spirits, wind, current of air or wind (supernatural), divine giftings, and generally that which is in the invisible realm.

Two things it does: First, it gives your spirit access to the spirit realm. So, in essence, it activates your five senses *in the Spirit.* **Seeing, hearing, touching, tasting** and **smelling** in the Spirit what is not physically/naturally detected – it may exist in spiritual form. Secondly, it gives you the ability to judge the *source* of what you are detecting in the spirit. God should be the source of information when it comes to interpreting the manifestations of **discerning of spirits**. I say this because the body of Christ has grown cold in areas, to where they look for spiritual understanding from the world or even witchcraft. Daniel 2:20-22 explains the mind of God stating, "… Blessed be the name of God forever and ever, for wisdom and might are His. And He changes the times and the seasons; He removes kings and raises up kings; *he gives wisdom to the wise and knowledge to those who have understanding. He reveals deep and secret things; He knows what is in the darkness, and light dwells with Him."*

So, to give you a sharper picture, your physical body has five senses. Without these senses, you are unable to experience and interact with the physical realm of the world around you. In the same way, your spirit, that is inside your mortal body, has five senses as well. This gives you the ability to experience and interact with the spirit realm. So, look at all five of your spiritual senses as gates or access points. Ok, now hold that thought.

Let's look at spiritual gifts. Any believer can walk in d*iscernment*. The continued use of it exercises the spiritual gift, which in turn produces spiritual maturity as seen in Hebrews 5:14: "But solid food belongs to those who are of full age, *that is,* those who by reason of use have their senses exercised to discern both good and evil." We must make sure that the Word of God is the measuring tool by which we weigh our experiences in the spirit realm. This prevents us from operating in error.

To See (Spiritual Sight)

- Seeing in the Spirit (Rev 1:10-13) When your spiritual eyes are open at the same time that your natural eyes are, and you are able to see the spirit and natural realm simultaneously. A good example is when John said that he was in the spirit and Christ began to give him great revelation through seeing directly into the spirit realm.
- Dreams (Daniel 2) Whole books and trainings have been developed on dreams and interpretation alone. It is one of the

more popular and sought-after topics in discernment. There are many types of dreams, but below, we will see a general and brief summary of what a dream is.

- You are asleep and receive images, messages, and movies from God. During Daniel's time, the king experienced a dream and God gave Daniel the exact same dream. Dreams will typically need to be interpreted. Some are clearer than others.
- Remember that God can give the interpretation, but He is not obligated to interpret every dream or vision to us. Timing is important to God. Your dream may come one day and, out of the blue, ten days or ten years later, come back to you with the full understanding. Remember that He is sovereign.
- Dreams can be from our own soulish realm due to a lot of cares or activity in our lives. We see this in Ecclesiastes 5:3. These dreams need no interpretation. It is our mind playing out fears and events.
- Dreams can be derived from the enemy and these also need no interpretation. However, many times you can be attacked or enticed by the enemy in a dream (or vision). If you know the operation of the demon (like a lustful dream), instead of interpreting the dream, call out the demon. Command it to cease its operation in your life and dreams, and to go in the name of Jesus. In other words, take authority.

- o Remember, *do not* go to worldly sources (mysticism or psychology) to "crack the code" to any dream.
- <u>Visions</u>- are typically literal and are not limited to us being awake. So, know that visions can also occur in your sleep.
  - o <u>Open vision</u> (Acts 9:10-16)- when you see images that superimpose what your eyes can see. Sometimes you are unable to see anything in the natural, only the vision you are experiencing. Some visions are interactive like the one cited here. Ananias could hear and speak with Christ our Lord back and forth.
  - o <u>Pictures</u>- Similar to having images or videos playing in your mind. You know exactly what you saw. However, while it was happening you viewed it in your mind like you would when recalling a memory.
  - o <u>Night Vision</u> (Job 33:15-16)- It is a vision while asleep. You will know that it is not a dream because it will feel very real as though you are walking through each scene. It will feel as though you are really there. And, just as Elihu mentions in Job, sometimes a deep sleep can come upon you or you may already be asleep.
- <u>Trances</u> (Acts 10:9-23)- Typically God shuts down most, if not all, your natural senses and you are able to see into the spirit realm or experience a vision. This can also be sleep induced and if you should try to awaken, you may be put back to sleep until the vision is over. We see this in Peter's vision of animals that were considered unclean.

April Moore

To Hear in the Spirit

    Most people believe that the "devil" can talk to you. We see cartoons or shows where there is a demon on one shoulder and an angel on the other, and they are both trying to convince the hearer to do either right or wrong. However, there are denominations, and even individual believers, who *know* that God placed His spirit inside of them (for what, they may not understand), but they may believe that God wouldn't *speak* to them. My question is how horrible would it be for a parent to give birth to or raise their child in the same household, help them, comfort them, and be present but *refuse to speak to them?* And, if they do believe the parent [God] will speak, it may only be on occasions of warning or danger. Moses was a man and a friend of God. The Holy Spirit rested on him, yet God spoke to him face to face on a regular basis (Exodus 33:11 and Numbers 12:8). And, no that is not only for him nor for only Old Testament times. In John 10:3-5, Jesus said that the sheep hear the shepherd's voice and is led by that voice. God cannot lead sheep unless they can hear from Him.

    I am taking a bit more time on this one because there are many strongholds, insecurities, and misunderstandings about something basic that God desires to do for each of us. I pray that your life will be full of the various manifestations of discernment. However, even if you never experience *any* of the others, God wants to speak to you!

- <u>Audibly</u> (Acts 9:1-7)- This is where you can audibly hear with your physical ears in the spirit realm. Paul's Damascus Road experience is an excellent example of this. Many people have not, and may not, experience this type of hearing but that does not mean it cannot happen.

- <u>Inward voice</u> is where you can hear within yourself what is being said in the spirit realm. This is how most of us hear the voice of God – He speaks directly to our spirit, and we can discern the voice of God and what He is speaking. There are several ways to be led into this type of discernment, but a primary one is through the Word of God. If God gives insight into your life after reading scriptures or the preached Word, you are hearing from God! Discernment gives the ability to hear God speaking directly to you.

Touch (Feel) and Taste (Ezekiel 3:1-3 & Rev 10:9-10)

- Ezekiel had a scroll and John had a book. They could both see, taste, eat, and feel it. Ezekiel saw it, but he also felt it in his belly and mouth, and it tasted sweet like honey. And, in Revelations, John took the little book from the angel so he could feel it. He tasted it and it was sweet as honey but felt bitter to his stomach.

Smell (2 Corinthians 2:14-16)

This scripture shows us that Christ in us manifests as a sweet-smelling aroma that is diffused to others. The word *manifest* (*phaneroo*) in this context means to lay bare, uncover or to reveal.

April Moore

So, something that is literally hidden in the spirit becomes uncovered while discerning it.

I have often wondered why our light can be so offensive to those that are in darkness without us doing anything except *being of Christ*. This scripture goes on to say, "For we are to God the **fragrance** of Christ among those who are being saved and among those who are perishing. To the one *we are* the **aroma** of death *leading* to death, and to the other the aroma of life *leading* to life…" Could it be that the spirits of others can sense not only our light but our **scent**? To one, it may be a joyful aroma and to the other a reminder of the death from an un-regenerated spirit in Christ. Thus, some may feel condemned without us ever saying a word to them of their state.

Detect or Judge (Acts 16:16-18)

You can, as Paul did, detect negative or positive motives, *and* the nature of the spirit behind various events regardless of what it appears to be in the natural. He did this with the slave girl that had a spirit of divination. She appeared to say all the right things, but he discerned the spirit and motive behind her announcement of them.

If you are unsure of the spiritual origin of something:

- Ask God to make sure your heart is not hardened to where you cannot see Him moving. It can increase your faith if what you are seeing is truth.
- Pray to ensure that you are not being deceived.

- Remember, ultimately, it is Him that you believe in...**not** in the sign, testimony, person, or spirit that you see.

Please note: With time, we certainly get better in determining the origin of what we discern. But, even when we have had all these experiences, it can sometimes be difficult to convince us when things are not from God. For example, if you hear something in the spirit, it may be difficult to determine if it was from God, from you, or the enemy. But, if it is clearly against what the Word says, you must disregard what you heard. Another example is hearing that someone else's spouse should be your spouse, or you hear words that are very condemning about yourself or others – not convicting but condemning or tormenting. These are either a product of your own soul or the enemy, or a combination of both. Think of it this way, many of us wonder if a dream is from God, ourselves, or the enemy but we should know that, with any operation of discernment, we should *ask God* to help us understand. The best way, as I stated before, is to weigh it against the Word of God.

Word of Knowledge

Gnosis (gno'-sis)- Insight

Insight (Dictionary)- the power or act of seeing into a situation, **or** the act or result of apprehending the inner nature of things, or of seeing intuitively.

The **word of knowledge** is knowledge spiritually obtained through facts and spiritual insight received from the Lord. This is again, God revealing His mind to us. The fact can also be known somewhere, just not known to you. It is a great tool by God to increase faith in others. For example, if you know something about me that you could not have known, I am more apt to believe the subsequent message from God coming through you.

This gift is most often confused with discernment and even prophecy. You know that it is not prophecy because it is dealing with something that *can* be known either past or present. Prophecy deals more so with the future. And, you know that it is not discernment because although you hear it from your Spirit, you are gaining information and deeper insight. For example, **discernment** lets you know the *origin* of the spirit (God, angelic, demonic or human) and is also a gateway that gives us access to the spirit realm. The **word of knowledge** will tell you *what kind* of spirit it is – an angel of healing, warrior angels, demonic spirit of perversion, etc.

Paul knew by discernment that the spirit within the girl in Acts 16 was an evil spirit, but the **word of knowledge** gave further insight and he knew that it was specifically a spirit of divination.

> *Now it happened, as we went to prayer, that a certain slave girl possessed with a spirit of divination met us, who brought her masters much profit by fortune-telling. This girl followed Paul and us, and cried out, saying, "These men are the servants of the Most-High God, who proclaim to us the way of salvation." And this she did for many days. But Paul, greatly annoyed, turned and said to the spirit, "I command you in the name of Jesus Christ to come out of her." And he came out that very hour. (Acts 16:16-18)*

There are several ways that the word of knowledge operates. You may be reading the Bible and you receive a deeper revelation of what the scripture means. It is like God is explaining it to you. In the same way, you may receive greater insight on how a scripture pertains to your life, a situation or someone you know. Another good example is something that I experience quite often. Someone may be explaining a situation in their life and you receive greater understanding of what is currently happening in their life. You may even understand the spiritual dynamics of the circumstances surrounding them. For example, someone tells you they are experiencing depression and you are instantly aware of the reason for the depression (which may be because of a situation, a demonic oppression or physical issue they are dealing with). God may even reveal details about the cause for the depression. This would be a **word of knowledge** because you would normally have no insight as to what could have caused it.

You can also receive a **word of knowledge** without having any other information to draw from. You may hear the name of someone's loved one as you are praying for them on a completely different matter. Or, you may see someone walk through the door and know that they are struggling with addiction without there being any outward clues.

What I find exciting as I train and help to activate people in their gifts is how many have been operating in them quite unaware. It is not unusual for someone to feel as though the gift is just normal for them and part of how they relate to people. Some believers don't realize that they are drawing information from the Lord directly from the spirit realm. And, quite honestly, the operation of the gifts should be just *that*...normal for a believer. Nonetheless, when we know that we are exercising our gifts, we can grow in them and use them to greater measure – you may see that you operate in a gift one way but would like to stretch yourself to use the same gift in a different way. Knowledge is definitely power!

Word of Wisdom

Sophia (so-fee'-ah)- Supernatural ability to take natural or spiritually derived information and explain what to do with that information. Spiritual wisdom is from God and it gives Biblical guidance, advisement, and the counsel of God. It also means skillful, in that you know how to accomplish something.

Wisdom- a wise attitude, belief, or course of action

- The **word of wisdom** explains strategies, consequences and gives divine answers to an issue faced.
- Divine direction for your life or the lives of others through reading Scripture.
- This divine wisdom also gives supernatural ability to those that have special natural skills
    - Examples: singers, artists, computer engineers, craftsmen, secretaries, etc.
- <u>Wisdom by divine inspiration</u>- When you articulate an answer to others and teach them *how to apply* what is known to produce results, you are speaking a **word of wisdom** as well. This may be given by divine inspiration in that God deposited

this wisdom into you – you know that you would not have known how to do this on your own.

Let's look at the scripture we used previously when studying **word of knowledge**. In Acts 16:16-18, we see again that Paul **discerned** that the spirit in the slave girl was evil. He knew by divine **knowledge** that it was a spirit of divination. And, by the **wisdom** gift in operation, he knew *how* to handle the situation.

Here's all three in action in the form of **dream interpretation**. Our study originates from New Testament Greek words; however, these gifts have been functioning for centuries before the New Testament was written.

Dream Interpretation

One of the most common questions I get is, "Is there a gift of dream or vision interpretation?" The answer is yes. Here is how a dream or vision can be dissected Biblically and interpreted. Let's look at Joseph and Daniel for example.

Study - Joseph Interprets Pharaoh's Dream: Genesis 41

- **Discernment-** God gave a dream to Pharaoh in Genesis 41:1-7, 15-24
- **Word of Knowledge-** Joseph could explain what each element or symbol of the dream meant – the corn, the cows and what it meant when the smaller ones ate the larger. Also, he

explained the fact that there were seven of these representing the seven years of plenty followed by seven years of famine (Genesis 41:26-32).
- **Word of Wisdom-** Now Joseph proceeds to advise Pharaoh on what to do with this information. He tells him to get a discerning and wise man, store twenty percent of the grain in the seven plentiful years, and so forth (Genesis 41:33-37).

Study Daniel's Dream: Daniel 1

- **Knowledge and Wisdom**- Daniel 1 says that He was filled with wisdom and had understanding (**knowledge**) in all visions and dreams. In Chapter 2, Daniel acknowledges that **wisdom** is from God.
- **Discernment-** King Nebuchadnezzar had the dream (Dan 2:3). He saw the images that God placed in his mind.
- **Discernment**- Daniel received a night vision (Dan 2:19) where God showed him what the King also saw. He thanked God for **knowledge** and **wisdom** (Dan 2:21-22). Acknowledges that God is the revealer of secrets (Dan 2:28-30).
- **Word of Knowledge**- The rest details how Daniel identified what each of the symbols of the statue meant, thereby interpreting the dream.

Journal Questions:

1. What are three things that stand out to you after reading this section of gifts?

2. Do you notice that you may have been operating in a certain area of discernment that you may not have noticed before?

3. After looking at the three gifts that we just covered, do you see areas of a gift in which you would like to grow?

April Moore

Inspirational Gifts

The *inspirational gifts* are also brought by revelation. In some circles, you will hear of these being included in with the *revelation gifts*. In other circles, they are called *utterance gifts*. Nevertheless, because the execution of these gifts is driven by the Holy Spirit differently, we will follow suit with yet another school of thought and call them the *inspirational gifts*. These are categories that teachers and theologians have assigned to explain the function. The gifts themselves are inspired utterances under the direction of the Holy Spirit just as God speaks. These gifts are the gift of **tongues,** the gift of **interpretation of tongues** and the gift of **prophecy**.

Tongues

Glossa (*gloce-sah*)- The way this word is used in the NT, it is an *unnaturally acquired tongue or language*. Note that this language in the NT is typically referred to as a language that exists but you have *no prior knowledge* of the language. Tongues is an amazing phenomenon in how it manifests and functions. There is one NT word that describes the gift of tongues, however there are many ways that this gift manifests.

Tongues as an Unknown Language

Divers- Genos (*ghen'-os*)- family, kindred, tribe or nation

- 1 Corinthians 12:10- "**divers** kinds of **tongues *[genos glossa]***"
- 1 Corinthians 12:28- "**diversities** of **tongues *[genos glossa]*** to edify the church"
- Acts 2:3-4- "Then there appeared to them divided **tongues *[glossa]*,** as of fire, and one sat upon each of them. And they were all filled with the Holy Spirit and began to speak with other ***tongues***, as the Spirit gave them utterance."

Tongues as a Prayer Language

To clarify ***glossa*** as a prayer language, it is the same phenomenon but with a different manifestation and function. You are part of the Kingdom of Heaven, so know that this type of **tongues** edifies (or builds) you spiritually. It can also cause things to happen in the spirit realm because, in its nature, it is prayer to God. You just may not, by natural means, know exactly *how* that is happening.

- 1 Corinthians 13:1- "Though I speak with the **tongues [glossa] of men and of angels…"**
    - The Greek for "men and angels" literally means men and angels. We can speak in an earthly known language (just unknown to you) or a heavenly language (a language you are speaking to God also known as your **prayer language**).
- 1 Corinthians 14:2- "For he who speaks in a **tongue [glossa]** does not speak to men but to God. For no one understands him, ***however in the spirit he speaks mysteries***."
- 1 Corinthians 14:4- "He who speaks in a **tongue [glossa]** edifies himself…"
- 1 Corinthians 14:14- "For if I pray in a **tongue [glossa]**, *my spirit prays*, but my mind is unfruitful."

Tongues as the Holy Spirit Praying Through You

This is the type of **tongues** that we often call a travail. Romans 8:26 (KJV) shows how the **Holy Spirit** makes intercession for us. And, *that* sounds like groanings not to be uttered. "Not to be uttered" in Greek means to be audibly heard but not spoken in **words**.

Typically, but not exclusively, you will find that intercessors will travail. Allowing the Holy Spirit to intercede through you is powerful and may often sound different. As you connect deeper in prayer, you will find that your prayers shift and may sound as though you are warring or rejoicing and even laughing. What is important is that you flow with the Spirit of God who is praying perfectly through you!

So, though in scripture throughout the passages it shows the word **tongues**, the original Greek word can give us greater understanding of the many ways it manifests.

Language- Dialektos (dee-al'-ek-tos)- means a naturally learned language or dialect. It is the **tongues** mentioned in Acts 2:8 meaning a tongue or language of a specific people (example: English, Italian, French, Swahili).

- Acts 2:8- "And how is it that we hear, each in our own **tongue [dialektos or language]** in which we were born?"

Interpretation of Tongues

Interpretation- hermeneia (her-may-ni-ah)- the explanation to the meaning of something.

Tongues- See previous section.

Interpretation of tongues is perhaps the most underutilized spiritual gift. I believe it has a lot to do with misunderstandings surrounding the gift. It is certainly not a gift that can be grasped *intellectually* before you operate in it. Some fear that the Holy Spirit will "take over" in a way that will embarrass them while many just don't believe in its operation at all...but all gifts operate by faith. In fact, the greater your faith, the more you are able to exercise any of the gifts.

In 1 Corinthians 14, we see Paul establishing order in how **interpretation of tongues** should operate in the church.

> *In the law it is written: 'With men of other tongues and other lips I will speak to this people; And yet, for all that, they will not hear Me says the Lord.'*
>
> *Therefore, tongues are for a sign, not to those who believe but to unbelievers; but prophesying is not for unbelievers but for those who believe. Therefore, if the whole church comes together in one place, and all speak with tongues, and there come in those who are uninformed or unbelievers, will they not say that you are out of your mind? But if all prophesy, and an unbeliever or an uninformed person comes in, he is convinced by all, he is convicted by all. And thus, the secrets of his heart are revealed; and so, falling down on his face, he will worship God and report that God is truly among you. (1 Corinthians 14:21-25)*

However, as the Holy Spirit can do absolutely anything, there are exceptions to this!

1. Example for unbeliever:
   In Acts 2, Pentecost, the men could supernaturally hear each in their own native language. These men were not yet believers.
   a. Example: A minister was able to preach and evangelize in another language, *without* an interpreter in a foreign earthly tongue.
2. Example for believer:
   A **tongue** (glossa) can go forth and the Holy Spirit will give the interpretation.

a. Example: A believer heard a woman praying in tongues and it was his native language. She did not know until he told her, and it was something that encouraged him.

Prophecy

Propheteia (prof-ay-ti'-ah)- to foretell future events. It also means to speak by divine inspiration, divine declaration, or divine utterance the counsel or mind of God. A deeper definition is:

> *A discourse emanating from divine inspiration and declaring the purposes of God, whether by reproving and admonishing the wicked, or comforting the afflicted or revealing things hidden; especially by foretelling future events (Thayer).*

There are different levels of anointing and responsibility that we view in scripture. The simple and most basic form of prophecy is mentioned in 1 Cor 14:3-4. This shows what our concentration is in prophesying and that it is available for any believer to walk in. A person in their prophetic or apostolic mantle or office would have more authority and responsibility to speak prophetically in addition to what is expressed in this scripture.

> *But one who prophesies speaks to men for edification and exhortation and consolation. One who speaks in a tongue edifies himself; but one who prophesies edifies the church (1 Corinthians 14:3-4).*

The result of the **prophecy** should bring edification, exhortation and/ or consolation.

- **Edification (oikodome)**- confirmation and the act of building up and promoting growth.
- **Exhortation (paraklesis)**- also means encouragement. A given persuasive discourse or stirring address. It can comfort or bring solace.
- **Consolation (paramuthia)**- A different word that is very similar to exhortation, in that it persuades, but it does so by a broader means. It can mean a stirring up or a calming or consoling address.

At times, it can sound like one is taking dictation for the Lord and speaking it. So, you may hear something like this:

- "The Lord wants to…" "The Lord is saying…" "This is what God is saying…" or, good old-fashioned, "Thus says the Lord…"

There may not even be an intro, or the intro may start as a discourse of some type and end up flowing into a prophecy like Zacharias in Luke 1 (which we will look at soon).

You are like an antenna and you are broadcasting what God is saying, so it is sometimes going to be in first person._Here is an example: The Lord is saying, "I will deliver you and protect you. Never will you go through this again. You will perceive My hand on your life as you walk out of the darkness, and never again will you doubt the magnitude of my glory." In this example, you see **comfort** and **foretelling** of something in the future.

Prophecy in Scripture

- <u>Nathan</u>- "He shall build Me a house, and I will establish his throne forever. I will be his Father, and he shall be My son; and I will not take My mercy away from him, as I took it from him who was before you" (1 Chronicles 17:12-13).
- <u>Gad, David's Seer</u>- "Now when David arose in the morning, the word of the LORD came to the prophet Gad, David's seer, saying, "Go and tell David, 'Thus says the LORD: "I offer you three *things;* choose one of them for yourself, that I may do *it* to you"'" (2 Samuel 24:11-12).
- <u>Zacharias</u>- "Now his father Zacharias was filled with the Holy Spirit, and prophesied, saying… "And you, child, will be called the prophet of the Highest; For you will go before the face of the Lord to prepare His ways, To give knowledge of salvation to His people By the remission of their sins, Through the tender mercy of our God, With which the Dayspring from on high has visited us; To give light to those who sit in darkness and the shadow of death, To guide our feet into the way of peace" (Luke 1:67,76-79).
    - Zacharias has just begun to speak again after the birth of his son John, whom we refer to as John the Baptist. This is an example in scripture where it starts as one type of discourse, in verse 68, but flows into a prophecy, in verse 76. We will study this later in the book.

April Moore

Prophetic Guidelines

- It is good, especially at first, to take someone with you when delivering a Word.
- This gift does not indicate that you are a prophet. All believers, by the unction of the Holy Spirit can prophesy.
- Though God can reveal His emotions to you about a thing, **we do not prophesy out of our <u>own</u> emotions.** This is one way to prophesy out of the soulish realm, or self. Submit your soul to God – your will, intellect and emotions. Yield to His emotions on the matter. Is He grieved, rejoicing, encouraging etc.?
- Prophecy is redemptive. Don't leave someone without hope or direction as to how God can redeem a situation. Press in to hear *all* of what God is saying about a situation.
- **Death, birth, marriage, divorce and negative prophecies should *usually* be delivered by the mature.** Or, have the Word submitted to someone with greater knowledge and wisdom (i.e. Prophet or an Elder). You want to make sure that you are supposed to deliver the Word or that you have accountability before delivering the Word. Mature Apostles and Prophets, for example, have an authority with their calling that may warrant them to release these types of words.
- Sometimes God is speaking but you are never to deliver the Word, *you are to pray*. Or, you may pray for a season prior to

delivering the Word. No matter how urgent it feels or how much it burns within you, know first if you should speak it. So, be a **witness** that brings confirmation to the word. God may reveal things to *several people* because witnesses are very important!

- Timing is everything. You don't want to deliver a Word out of season. You may need to pray further into a Word the Lord is speaking to you.
- We are careful not to lift ourselves up because of gifting. <u>You are not special</u> because you prophesy or walk in giftings. <u>You are special</u> because you are His.
- **Do not sit** on a word you know you should deliver, and **be cautious** to move when you are unsure. God is more interested in you handling His word with respect and care.
- You are going to make mistakes sometimes.

April Moore

Journal Questions:

1. Have you ever spoken in tongues? If so, which function of tongues have you experienced (prayer, unknown language or Holy Spirit interceding)? Explain some of your direct or indirect experiences.

2. Why do you think interpretation of tongues is not often exercised?

3. What are some new things you learned about prophecy after reading this passage?

4. What are some of the questions you still have about prophecy?

5. The list of guidelines is not exhaustive. Can you think of other prophetic guidelines?

Power Gifts

The Power Gifts display God's power through man under the direction of the Holy Spirit as God wills. These gifts are the **gift of faith**, the **gift of healings** and the **gift of working miracles**.

April Moore

Faith

Pistis (pis'-tis)- a conviction of the truth, a persuasion, assurance, and belief as it pertains to God and the Kingdom of God. Faith can also be executed outwardly in the act of persuading.

> Now **faith** is the substance of things hoped for, the evidence of things not seen. For by it the elders obtained a good testimony. By **faith** we understand that the worlds were framed by the word of God, so that the things which are seen were not made of things which are visible (Hebrews 11:1-3).

- This faith is based on the Word of God (written or spoken Word). It is not **faith** that is based on our own soulish beliefs. It is **faith** that is activated by the power of God and goes beyond human limitations of belief.
- It has no doubt or unbelief. It is **faith** that declares that what you are believing God for already exists, and to you, it may because it feels *that* real.
- Faith makes what you are believing **real** in a way that cannot be seen.
- We can see from this scripture that faith is a placeholder and a building block for what you are believing God for.
- There is power in faith-filled words – to stir up the atmosphere around you and bring to pass that which is declared. We see this with those that speak faith confessions and declarations.

See this in your mind

You are believing God for something special to manifest that does not yet exist in the natural. So, your **faith** looks like an invisible group of bricks sitting next to you that only you can see. What you are believing God for exists *in the spirit realm* because it is something that God promised you (directly, or in His Word). Your **faith** says, "I know for sure that it is already here!" Why? Because your faith makes it real. It gives natural substance to what you are believing for. **Faith** also creates a vacuum so that it attracts what you are believing God for – it gives legal rights for it to exist here. God's power drives it from one realm to the other. Simply put, exercising **faith** is an exercise of **authority**.

God determines the "shipping method" and timeframe

By believing, you are saying, "Yes God, I do want it here," but, the manifestation can take seconds or years to manifest. God's sovereignty will ensure that your "package" arrives within the seasonal window that *He* has determined, if you will only believe and be of good courage.

> *Therefore, do not cast away your confidence, which has great reward. For you have need of endurance, so that after you have done the will of God, you may receive the promise:*
>
> *"For yet a little while, And He who is coming will come and will not tarry. Now the just shall live by faith; But if anyone draws back, my soul has no pleasure in him." (Hebrew 10:35-38)*

April Moore

Faith is also a precursor for all other gifts to operate

The power, utterance gifts and revelation gifts, and *every other gift* that will be mentioned in this book, all in some way operate through **faith**. In the testimony of the centurion's servant (Matthew 8:5-13), Jesus said "...I have not found such **great faith**, not even in Israel! Go your way, and **as you have believed**, so let it be done for you." Healing can come for you *just as it did* for the centurion's servant.

Faith will not go against the wisdom of God. They give balance to each other. Wisdom establishes Kingdom order, so why would God go against something that He established? Here is the dividing line: God's wisdom may require a leap of faith which can appear unwise to some. But, since God does want us to work inside of order, He decides when those leaps occur. We do not otherwise we are in danger of falling into error. We operate inside of established order until He speaks to us differently. This is common especially in young believers. Some will have faith for something, while another will look at the activation of that faith as foolish. Moreover, there are still those that have great wisdom but will negate the **freedom of faith**. A faith journey can be a lonely journey if no one else sees what you see. Thought can be that maybe the wise one is actually right, or maybe the faith-filled person is. Remember, we can "miss it" in the activation of any gifting. Here is a litmus test. If it is against the Word of God, then you *know* for sure that it is *not* God-centered faith. Example: Believing that God said a man or woman is your spouse when they are married to someone else. This is dangerous and rooted in witchcraft, not God. So, be careful how you believe and find Biblical precedence (a scripture) that backs your faith. Or, ask yourself if God spoke a personal promise to you.

In 2001, the Lord gave me the name and vision of Kingdom Enlightenment Ministries, based on Ephesians 1:15-23. I wanted to give people, not a church perspective of Christianity, but a Kingdom and Christ perspective of our Bridal call and dominion in Him. I wanted to really raise up believers that are intense lovers of God and full of His glory and dominion – who can open gates for God to reign on this earth through us who are in Christ. It took about 17 years or increasing, learning, deliverance, warfare, tears, study, observation, heartache, discouragement, encouragement, strength… and increased unshakable faith for it to manifest. This is what faith looked like in my life. People didn't readily see the God deposits in me because it was not time. I had a promise that no one around me could comprehend. But I stood so others can stand.

Holding on to promises from God increases your capacity for faith! This not only insures or helps to ensure that your faith is solid, but it also helps *you* to stand when things begin to appear contrary to the Word you received and are standing on!

April Moore

Healings

Iama (ee'-am-ah)- healing or a cure.

Note that the Word of God says *healings*, meaning the healing manifests supernaturally and it is not limited to the physical body; it can be healing of the soul (emotional healing, trauma and brokenness).

Healing of the Spirit (Eph 2:2 & Cor 5:17)

Before salvation, our spirit is dead in sin. Through the confession of our **faith**, Christ gifts us with salvation. Salvation regenerates and renews our spirit and makes our spirit alive in Christ. It is then perfected and made new in Him. ***Basically, our spirit is resurrected from the dead.***

Healing of the Soul (emotion, intellect and will)

- Emotional healing- (Psalm 147:3) He heals the brokenhearted and binds up their wounds.
- Intellectual healing (Romans 12:2) Daily renewing your mind or *nous* (pronounced "nooce") meaning intellect.
- Healing of the will (Luke 9:23) Yielding to Christ; Denying yourself and following Christ.

Healing of the body

One example of physical healing is in Acts 3, when Peter healed the lame man at the gate called Beautiful. Also, there is Mark 6:54-56, where Jesus healed those that were sick when they touched his garment:

> *And when they came out of the boat, immediately the people recognized Him, ran through that whole surrounding region, and began to carry about on beds those who were sick to wherever they heard He was. Wherever He entered, into villages, cities, or the country, they laid the sick in the marketplaces, and begged Him that they might just touch the hem of His garment. And as many as touched Him were made well.*

Working of Miracles

Working- Energema (en-erg'-ay-mah)- Something created or an operation.

Miracle- Dunamis (doo'-nam-is)- Abundance of ability, mighty deed, strength, violence, mighty wonderful work. Inherent power, moral power and excellence of soul (meaning on the side of righteousness), power that rests or resides in armies, forces or hosts.

A miracle can change the forces of nature and manifest in:

- Weather (1 Kings 17-19)- Elijah stopped rain from falling and it didn't rain for 3½ years. Then, he prayed for rain and suddenly there was a downpour.
- Defying Physics (Matt. 14:22-33)- Jesus and Peter walking on water.
- Halting Time (Joshua 10:12-14)- The sun stood still.

April Moore

- <u>Changing Chemical & Physical Properties</u> (John 2:7-10)- Turning water into wine.
- <u>Divine Multiplication</u> (Matt. 14:17-21)- Multiplying fish and loaves
- <u>Supernatural Physical Power</u> (Judges 16:3)- Sampson took the doors of the city gate and its posts and carried it all away on his shoulders.
- And more…

With God there's always more! For example, Sampson wasn't the only one that manifested supernatural strength and agility. We see in 2 Samuel 23:8-39 that there were three top mighty men and thirty-four others in David's company:

- <u>Josheb-Basshebeth, the Tachmonite</u>- "…he had killed eight hundred men **at one time**."
- <u>Eleazar</u>- "…one of the three mighty men with David when they defied the Philistines *who* were gathered there for battle, **and the men of Israel had retreated**. He arose and attacked the Philistines until his hand was weary, and his hand stuck to the sword. **The Lord brought about a great victory that day**; and the people returned after him only to plunder.
- <u>Shammah</u>- "The Philistines had gathered together into a troop where there was a piece of ground full of lentils. **So, the people fled from the Philistines**. But he stationed himself in the middle of the field, defended it, and killed the Philistines. **So, the Lord brought about a great victory**."

Other Examples of Ways Power Gifts Can Manifest:

- <u>Laying on of hands</u> (1 Timothy 4:14)- God can use our hands to do mighty things! Timothy's gifts were stirred up and brought forth by a power punch combination of prophecy (which **spoke** forth the gift in Timothy) and laying on of hands (which **brought** forth the gift). *Hand* in the Greek here is ***cheir (khire)*** which literally means putting on hands, but also indicates **power**. Another application is that during the laying on of hands, the Holy Spirit is manifesting His **power** in the form of an answer that is needed by the recipient. He is being imparted into them by greater measure...and sometimes overwhelming the receiver. As we can see here in 1 Timothy, gifts are being stirred up, but the purposes and manifestations of the Holy Spirit in our lives are endless.
- <u>With objects</u> (Exodus 4)- It was miraculous when God instructed Moses to throw his staff on the ground and it became a serpent.
- <u>Shadows</u> (Acts 5:15)- The shadow of Peter brought healing to all that it fell upon.
- <u>Obedience to God's instruction</u>- Just as we saw in previously mentioned scriptures, Jesus **directed** the disciples on what to do with the fish and bread loaves. Also, when He **instructed** the servants to pour water into the water pots and then the water turned to wine. In this case, He never touched the water; the servants simply **obeyed**.

April Moore

Things to Remember

- **Proverbs 18:16** says that your gifts will make room for you and bring you before great men. We do not manipulate, push our way or demand to use them. That can be difficult when hope is deferred, and you have waited a long time. It can also be difficult when you are in upper leadership and have great vision to do more. Remember that everyone is under authority and must be released as God gives you release. From smallest to greatest, **we do not make or demand our way** into position or to utilize our gifting. It is not done by force, but by submission.
- Don't be discouraged when your gifts are not seen by leadership. God will hide you at times, as He is developing other areas of your life, even when you may not be aware. If the fullness were to be immediately revealed, you may be pushed before it is time. In the meantime, pray that God will open the way for you in *His* time.
- It is the grace of God when He minimizes some gifts in order to develop your character. He may want you to focus more on getting yourself ready as a willing vessel, fit for duty in the kingdom. It is a good thing to get "benched" at times so that you are not ministering from a contaminated place. Those that are used despite troubled areas they are dealing with, run the risk of becoming prideful/arrogant, having a seared conscience and unable to see their error.

- Never minister just to get a Word for people without it penetrating **your heart first**.

April Moore

Journal Questions:

1. People often face the dilemma that wisdom and faith can conflict. What are ways you have experienced this or seen it happen in someone else's life?

2. Have you seen or experienced supernatural healing? If not, is it something that you are interested in seeing God do? Why or why not?

3. Do you believe that miracles still happen today? Explore in your journal thoughts you have about that.

CHAPTER 4

Chapter 4 - The Design Gifts

In earlier writings, I referred to these gifts as **service gifts**. However, they are more accurately described as **design gifts**. These gifts are often overlooked in scripture, possibly because they are a bit more scattered in the way they are documented versus the other gifts mentioned in this book. However, they are extremely important in the functioning of the Kingdom. Note that I said Kingdom and not church, because, again, all gifts should not be confined to the four walls of a sanctuary. They are for the people of God to function in daily, as salt and light wherever they go. Easily, these gifts translate into everyday life and even the marketplace. This is why I have called them **design gifts,** because they are gifts that speak to the design of a person. You can see them naturally occurring as soon as a child begins to function in the world. They are innate design gifts given by God that operate **regardless of the person having accepted**

salvation or not. The design of the person will activate these giftings.

These unique giftings often show up undetected as a supernatural phenomenon. Many will simply appear to be a great trait. But make no mistake, the following gifts are just as powerful as any other. These gifts are also easily utilized in many different platforms, arenas and settings. They can be used in ways the world can easily relate to and recognize. They also go beyond what you see and are clearly the innate anointing of God at work. In fact, they are attributes of God Himself and He chose to infuse each of us with some, or several, of these gifts in fabric of our being.

*I highlighted the gifts that pertain to **design** in the following supporting scripture. Brackets were added for clarification.* **Prophecy** *and* **faith** *were covered under the Gifts of the Holy Spirit.*

> Having then gifts differing according to the grace that is given to us, let us use them: if prophecy, let us prophesy in proportion to our faith; or ministry [service], let us use it in our ministering; he who teaches, in teaching; he who exhorts, in exhortation; he who gives, with liberality; he who leads, with diligence; he who shows mercy, with cheerfulness" (Romans 12:6-8).

Gifts show up again in 1 Corinthians 12:27-28:

> Now you are the body of Christ, and members individually. And God has appointed these in the church: first apostles, second prophets, third teachers, after that miracles, then gifts of healings, **helps, administrations**, varieties of tongues.

IMPORTANT WARNING

This warning could go for **any** of the gifts explained in this book, but the following gifts deserve a warning even more so because they are not often realized as even being gifts. They are imbedded in the **design of the individual**. So, people may be unaware that they are even flowing in them.

It is *very* important to note that we can choose to operate in these gifts in self-strength or we can choose to submit them to God. In other words, submit your design to the Lord and allow Him to show you how to administrate your gift. Why is this important? Because, self-strength leads to burnout and even feeling taken advantage of. Many people will walk away from their design because they will become tired of the administration of their design failing. Here is a scenario:

> Laney is a **giver**. She will often feel compelled to give to others without even thinking about it. Immediately, she looks for resources and ways to give to someone or a cause in need. But, when the gift is squandered by others or people keep coming to her, or manipulating her into giving, she feels used. Over time, she wants to stop giving altogether. Once she starts shutting down or pulling back from her **design**, she feels as though a piece of her has died and bitterness or indifference sets in. Darkness begins to fill this part of her design and she may even start making inner vows to never give to people in that way again. So now when she feels compelled to give, she shuts it down and loses part of herself.

This isn't only for the **giver**, it applies to any of the **design gifts**. The key to managing a **design gift** is by submitting it to God. Seek God and partner *with Him* in your design! Since it is a part of *His nature*, He wants to show you how to implement it the way He would. This protects you and gives you greater insight. **Always remember** that God wants to increase the wisdom in you concerning your **design,** and that there is no lost experience in Christ. What you do, and go through, matters and He wants to use it all. You won't always get it right, and He is ok with that as long as you are committed to learn.

April Moore

Here are just a few questions you can ask God:
1. Should I take action?
2. If so, how should I take action?
3. God, what are you wanting to produce in this situation?
4. Who are you wanting to touch?
5. Is there something I don't see or perceive before operating in my design in this area?
6. What wisdom should I learn while operating in this?

When you choose to partner with God in your design, it opens you up to a greater revelation of *who He is* and *who you are in Him*. This is the foundation of our identity in Christ. To know and be known by Him. When you walk with God in your design, it is a beautiful experience. You are free to be yourself and touch the world with who you are, which comes from the fabric of God. You begin to understand that you are a work in progress and there is a **reason** He wants you to be part of this world.

My Charge to You

So, I release you all to be the **design** of God imparted in the earth! You have gifts and *you are* a gift, first to Him and also to others!

Administration

Kubernesis (koo-ber'-nay-sis)- government, governing, or direction. *Kubernesis* gets its roots from a Latin word meaning to steer, pilot or to captain. In this very goal-oriented and authoritative gift, one would be able to navigate and direct ministries, projects and tasks.

Joseph was an excellent example of someone who operated in **administration**. He was first made overseer of the house of Potiphar in Genesis 39. His gift was so dynamic, that even as a prisoner himself, he was entrusted over all matters concerning the other prisoners. Genesis 39:20-23 says:

> *Then Joseph's master took him and put him into the prison, a place where the king's prisoners were confined. And he was there in the prison. But the Lord was with Joseph and showed him mercy, and He gave him favor in the sight of the keeper of the prison. And the keeper of the prison committed to Joseph's hand all the prisoners who were in the prison; whatever they did there, it was his doing. The keeper of the prison did not look into anything that was under Joseph's authority, because the Lord was with him; and whatever he did, the Lord made it prosper.*

Gift Attributes

These are people that like to create efficient systems or make existing systems and processes more efficient. They are good at managing projects and can also see the importance in details – details that others may discount as irrelevant. They intuitively see an issue, create a plan of action, and bring resolutions to problems. Because they are project oriented and organizers, in their more mature state, they see the value in delegating responsibilities to others.

Leadership

Proistemi (pro-is'-tay-mee)- to be diligent in leading, to set over, or exercise care over others. Leadership is somewhat similar to the administration gift in that it means one leads, rules and sets in place. However, instead of presiding over a goal or task, the **focus is on people**.

These people lead with the heart for people and are in some form like a guardian to them. A great example of that was Moses. He was a prophet but also very much a caring leader to the people of God. As he heard from the Lord, he could motivate and guide people the way God wanted them to go. When he needed a better process for hearing and meeting the needs of the people, Jethro showed him a more efficient way to carry out the plan. We also see, in the book of Exodus, how he cared for the people and went to God when the people needed something. And, he also gave the instructions of the Lord when provisions were made. More of his story is in Exodus chapters 13, 14, and 18.

Gift Attributes

These people are easily labeled or viewed as visionaries or dreamers. They see the big picture in any framework they are placed in. What I mean is, whether it is a church, ministry, their home life, relationships, or job, they see the broader vision. They may not necessarily know *how* to get there (unless they have a gift mix with perhaps an administrative gift). Because they see things from afar, and believe so deeply in the vision, they are often risk takers. They are not afraid to lead people, even in crisis. Details of how to get somewhere may frustrate this person and cloud their view. They are wired to see broader sweeping strokes than the minute details of a thing. Again, if they have other gift mixes that balance some of these frustrations, it can be a help. Even if they have people around them that can bring balance, it will greatly help this person to excel in even their own visionary efforts. Also, these people are such great natural leaders of people that they can spot another leader and motivate them to action.

Exhortation

Parakaleo (par-ak-al-eh-o')- a call to action; the type of communication that stirs up, convicts, and excites us to move or produce something. Exhortation does this in many ways including, consoling, comforting, and reprimanding.

When this gift is exercised, the goal is **to build up others**. One reference mentioned earlier (in the inspiration gifts) was concerning Zacharias after the birth of his son, John the Baptist. What he speaks starts out with an **exhortation** and ends with prophecy. It reads much like a psalm, in that it glorifies God and you can almost hear Zacharias preaching this with zeal and enthusiasm. He proclaims all

April Moore

that God has done for them and what He is doing. Here is the exhortation:

> Blessed is the Lord God of Israel for He has visited and redeemed His people, And has raised up a horn of salvation for us In the house of His servant David, As He spoke by the mouth of His holy prophets, Who have been since the world began, That we should be saved from our enemies and from the hand of all who hate us, To perform the mercy promised to our fathers and to remember His holy covenant, The oath which He swore to our father Abraham: To grant us that we, Being delivered from the hand of our enemies, Might serve Him without fear, In holiness and righteousness before Him all the days of our life. (Luke 1:68-75)

Gift Attributes

The **exhorter** is gifted to call people to action! They are big encouragers, and truly want to see the countenances of people lifted. They can motivate people to regain focus and get back up and follow God again. If you need a boost in the morale of a group, simply put an exhorter in the center of the room and the mindset of the whole room can be shifted. The gift of **faith** packaged in words from an **exhorter's** mouth brings powerful impartation!

Teaching

Didasko (did-as'-ko)- to instruct or give instruction.

While teaching, you are explaining things so that others can easily understand. Teaching the Bible and Biblical concepts can greatly influence the minds and direction of others. So, teaching is simply imparting knowledge to others and can be done in various ways. Note that it is the *gift level* of teaching. More will be discussed on teaching as an ascension gift/calling.

Jesus did everything, and teaching was one of His specialties. His teaching was revolutionary! He taught people how to live, what to look forward to and He changed the way many people thought about God. His teachings were important to the formation of Christianity today. One example of a revolutionary teaching, that many of us have become familiar with today, is Matthew 5:43-46:

> *You have heard that it was said, 'You shall love your neighbor and hate your enemy. But I say to you, love your enemies, bless those who curse you, do good to those who hate you, and pray for those who spitefully use you and persecute you, that you may be sons of your Father in heaven; for He makes His sun rise on the evil and on the good, and sends rain on the just and on the unjust. For if you love those who love you, what reward have you? Do not even the tax collectors do the same?*

This is revolutionary because when Jesus arrived, He brought reformation and He fulfilled the law. No longer was the teaching of the day centered around separation, punishment, and concepts that said you give an eye for an eye. He fulfilled the law through the love of God. He gave man the power to love beyond sin and to encourage unification in the Body.

Gift Attributes

When the Word of God or Biblical concepts become too difficult to understand, a **teacher** is the person to run to. They love giving explanations to the questions and ponderings of others and are also able to **simplify complicated concepts**. In a healthy and whole state, this person has a nose for error. Innately, they can sniff out false teaching. The redeemed teacher desires for others to have

April Moore

intimate knowledge of the Word of God so, as **catalysts of transformation**, they encourage others to dive deeper into the Word of God.

Mercy

Eleeo (el-eh-eh'-o)- to have compassion and empathy to help those afflicted by negative circumstance; to bring aid to those that have sinned.

This is an extremely important and defining gift for the New Testament Church. It is also a gift that is misunderstood in very religious-minded Christian groups. I believe God gave this gift to deposit His heart and nature within us all, especially for Kingdom-minded people. Remember, unlike the gifts found in other chapters, these gifts are a part of **human design**. They are not contingent upon salvation. These attributes can be in any number of Christians and non-Christians alike.

Mercy is often confused with **grace**. As we stated in chapter 1, **grace *(charis)*** means God's good will toward us, His kindness, beneficial favor, and gift. You can view **grace** as being an outward expression or gift from God, while **mercy** is more of an inward pardon of sin and flaw of character. But it is followed by an action that brings aid. They are different operations. We may be graced (endowed as a gift) to extend **mercy** to those that many would not feel deserve it.

In the Parable of the *Unforgiving Servant*, found in Matthew 18:21-35, we see God's heart when we do not show mercy to others. He is merciful and wants the same for us. Verses 33-35, in particular, give a strong warning about lacking compassion when it is in our power to do so.

> Should you not also have had compassion on your fellow servant, just as I had pity on you?' And his master was angry and delivered him to the torturers until he should pay all that was due to him. "So My heavenly Father also will do to you if each of you, from his heart, does not forgive his brother his trespasses. (Matthew 18:33-35)

Gift Attributes

Those with the design gift of **mercy** are definitely in touch with the feelings and well-being of others. Because empathy and feeling the burdens of others can be heavy, the Bible instructs, in Romans 12:8, that when we show mercy, do it with cheerfulness. Why does it say with cheerfulness? Well, people that feel **mercy** can often feel heavy. Nonetheless, if they focus on God's light, hope, restoration, and redemption, it will lift their countenance knowing that their help causes a ripple effect to restore the joy of another. People with this gift may express their feelings through actions that bring joy, restoration, and hope to those afflicted. **Condemnation is far from their mind.** While they understand sin and the penalty, they often want to **protect** people from it and bring them to restoration.

April Moore

Giving

Metadidomi (met-ad-id'-o-mee)- to share or impart.

This definition lends itself to sharing or giving of anything in your possession – natural goods, service and even sharing through communication. This is important because without the desire to give or impart to others, we can become selfish with the other gifts – deciding who can or should receive, based on personal preference and not the prompting of the Holy Spirit. Anyone can give, however as a **gift,** it is an extraordinary desire to give of one's self and resources.

Every gift has to be tempered with wisdom and this gift is no exception. For example, unless God very specifically says that you should do this because He will bless you shortly, I would not give money for my car note to another. God still requires us to steward our resources and our giving. This gift of **giving** is beautiful, and with wisdom, people with this **design** can give in great proportions. They may be able to motivate others to help by giving to causes as well.

Luke 3:11 gives a great selfless perspective of the gift of **giving**: "He answered and said to them, "He who has two tunics, let him *give* to him who has none; and he who has food, let him do likewise.""

Gift Attributes

A **giver** will often give above tithes and offering, but they are not limited to giving their money. They also give of their time and resources. **They have a clear revelation of giving being a Kingdom service** and will look for ways to cheerfully give, even if they have limited resources. Givers also desire to **locate resources** in order to share with others, regardless of personal need. And, they are called to **great stewardship**.

Helps/Service

These two gifts are closely related.

Helps- Antilepsis (an-til'-ape-sis)- in general, to bring aid.

Service- Diakonia (dee-ak-on-ee-ah)- either service or ministry (we will look at the ministry aspect of service in the next chapter). Service means to fulfil a request, command or a need for others. It also refers to meeting needs through charitable acts or food preparation.

People gifted in **helps** want to cater to the needs and give assistance to those who are seeking. In a church atmosphere, **helps** flows strong in those that are involved in outreach, ushers or sanctuary assistants. Those with a strong **administrative gift** coupled with **helps** may see that someone has a tremendous need and rally the troops to get it met. Or, they may develop systems to meet the needs of people on a larger scale. It is difficult for this person if they cannot meet a need because they are so driven to want to help people in any way they can. Below, is the *Parable of the Good Samaritan*, which shows different giftings at work, including **mercy**, **giving**, and **helps/service.**

> Then Jesus answered and said: "A certain man went down from Jerusalem to Jericho, and fell among thieves, who stripped him of his clothing, wounded him, and departed, leaving him half dead. Now by chance a certain priest came down that road. And when he saw him, he passed by on the other side. Likewise, a Levite, when he arrived at the place, came and looked, and passed by on the other side. But a certain Samaritan, as he journeyed, came where he was. And when he saw him, he had compassion. So, he went to him and bandaged his wounds, pouring on oil and wine; and he set him on his own animal, brought him to an inn, and **took care** of him. On the next day, when he departed, he took out two denarii, gave them to the innkeeper, and said to him, 'Take care of him; and whatever more you spend, when I come again, I will repay you.' (Luke 10:30-35)

Gift Attributes

Those with the design gift of **helps** will see significance in doing what others may see as insignificant, menial, or mundane. They not only have an eye for the needs of people and organizations, they seek to **meet the need**. Many times, a **giver** will shy away from recognition for service and the like – they want to serve behind the scenes. Another attribute is that they love to volunteer to meet practical needs and find fulfilment in helping others in these ways.

Possible Career Paths

Here are job examples, based on the mature and uncorrupted form, of each of the **design gifts**:

- **Administration-** Project Management, Executive Administrator, Facility Management, COO
- **Leadership-** CEO, Educational Administrators, Team Leaders
- **Exhortation-** Trainers, Politicians, Life Coaches, Lawyers
- **Teacher-** Instructor, Benefits Coordinator, Trainers
- **Mercy-** Correctional Officers, Social Workers, Case Managers
- **Giving-** Teachers (they impart), Philanthropists, Financial Consultants (they are skilled in financial wisdom)
- **Helps/Service-** Community involvement positions, Police, Military, City Counsel, Judges

April Moore

Journal Questions:

1. What are the top 3-4 design gifts that you see operating in your life?

2. Did you think these were random talents rather than actual spiritual gifts? Explain your answer.

3. Now that you view them as spiritual gifts how do you see yourself and your gifts?

4. Do you see how your service gifts can open the door for you to be a blessing in the marketplace or your realm of influence (school, job, business, etc.)? If so, in what ways?

CHAPTER 5

Chapter 5 – Callings

> *But to each one of us grace was given according to the measure of Christ's gift. Therefore, He says: 'When He ascended on high, He led captivity captive, and gave gifts to men.' (Now this, '**He ascended**'—what does it mean but that He also first descended into the lower parts of the earth? He who descended is also the One who ascended far above all the heavens, that He might fill all things.) And He Himself gave some to be apostles, some prophets, some evangelists, and some pastors and teachers. (Ephesians 4:7-15)*

When Christ ascended, He gave the ascension gifts. **The purpose of the ascension gifts is in verses 12-15 but most often the focus is on verse 12 alone.** So, let us look at this in the Amplified Version (which incorporates translated meaning from the original language):

> *...[and He did this] to fully equip and perfect the saints (God's people) for works of service, to build up the body of Christ [the church]; until we all reach oneness in the faith and in the knowledge of the Son of God, [growing spiritually]* <u>***to become a mature believer, reaching to the measure of the fullness of Christ [manifesting His spiritual completeness and exercising our spiritual gifts in unity]. So that we are no longer children [spiritually immature], tossed back and forth [like ships on a stormy sea] and carried about by every wind of [shifting] doctrine,***</u>

> **_by the cunning and trickery of [unscrupulous] men, by the deceitful scheming of people ready to do anything_** *[for personal profit]. But speaking the truth in love [in all things—both our speech and our lives expressing His truth], let us grow up in all things into Him [following His example] who is the Head—Christ. (Ephesians 4:12-15)*

As you can see from the Word of God, there is much work to be done. We cannot ignore or become afraid of these gifts. People must be **trained and activated** in these giftings. We have yet to see a wide-spread movement of the body of Christ equipping saints for maturity **and** unified in faith, etc. Men and women of God that have **ascension giftings** not only impart the gifts, they essentially embody and **become the gift** and serve as God leads them. They also establish God's **government** in the Earth to legislate and **build** according to God's design – as it pertains to the mantle they carry.

Terminology

An **ascension gift** is also what we refer to as a 5-Fold calling, or ministry gift. You may also see the words **mantle** and **office** mentioned.

Ascension gift, 5-Fold calling, office, governmental gift, 5-Fold mantle, and governmental mantle can be used synonymously. The terms have Biblical roots either expressly or through demonstration. They are used to refer to the **apostle**, **prophet**, **teacher**, **evangelist,** and **pastor**. *5-fold calling* is a manmade terminology that is very popular and in use in many circles. In the case of the local church, when your **governmental mantle** is found to be useful and needed in the local body, and you are recognized by your leadership to have that ascension gift, you may be ordained or commissioned into the **office** of that ascension gift. Commissioning into an **office** can also happen when your leadership is releasing you to start your own church or ministry (where you'll be operating in your **ascension gift**). I have written the book *Arising Governmental Mantles*, and the actual function of these ascension gifts are discussed more in depth there.

How do you know you are called?

I hear this often and there are many ways to answer this question. The reality is there are *thousands* and maybe *millions* of things God can <u>call</u> you to do! But there are only five ascension gifts,

April Moore

which is our focus for this chapter. Either God *tells* you, *leads* you into finding your calling, or your spiritual leader may see the gift on your life. And, that is the short answer.

Unlike all other spiritual gifts, an ascension gift is something that you are born with. Over time, it is revealed to you by God. It is not something you can desire to attain. It is not the summation or formula of other gifts that point to you having an ascension gift. And if you are called, usually you don't become that gift at the time of the call. It is through a series of "yeses" and process that are you chosen to come into the office of your ascension gift. Here is an example:

> *Before I formed you in the womb, I knew you, and before you were born, I consecrated you; I have appointed you a prophet to the nations. (Jeremiah 1:5)*

There are many ways that God may reveal an ascension gift to you. It is really easy for some to get rigid in this area, feeling that it should happen one way or another. But some were not exposed to the terminology of the 5-Fold or ascension gift ministry and may not know what it all entails. Instead, they may simply take notice that there are certain traits and attributes that seem different than the norm of what's around them. As they develop and study the ascension gifts, just like any other gift, they will begin to understand who they are, more and more. I have known some that received their calling in a combination of ways – their leader saw the calling already in operation, and as they began to research and study the calling, it all made sense to them. Also, God can speak to you and you can hear Him calling you into an **ascension gift**. There is no specific way to receive a calling, but you do want to make sure that what your leaders perceive as your calling, *really is* something God is **confirming in you**. However, once we are called, we should search out how to develop the **ascension gift**.

Gift-Level Anointing vs Calling

The teacher calling vs teaching as a gift and prophet calling vs prophecy are two giftings that show us there are levels to an anointing. One may have a **gift-level** to teach and one may be an **ascension gift teacher**. And still, another may have a gift to prophesy, and another may be a prophet. Remember, no one is greater, but the anointing may be such that it is designed to have a greater impact, territory, responsibility, and authority. This is important, because **all** Spirit-filled believers can be apostolic, prophetic, evangelistic, pastoral or teach in some capacity, but an ascension gift helps equip from their **mantle**. A simple way to look at it is, the ascension gift minister helps us to mature in those areas that they specialize in, or they will serve the people of God with their gift to bring them to **maturity**.

We should function in our gifts not only inside the church but also outside of the church walls. This is how we become **salt** (which is a preserver) to a deteriorating world and how we become **light** to a dark and fallen humanity. Remember that Ephesians 4:12 says the purpose of those with callings is "for the equipping of the saints for the work of ministry, for the edifying of the body of Christ." So, for

April Moore

example, the prophet will help others to be more prophetic. They may lead others to better understand the spirit realm, dreams, visions, prophecy, worship, intercession etc....depending on their focus or responsibilities as a prophet. Also, they may equip you by imparting into you. A prophet's impartation can help mature you by speaking a Word from the Lord to encourage you, give a word of rebuke, or warning. There is also a **governing** attribute of every ascension gift, and that is explained more in my book, *Arising Governmental Mantles*.

Ascension Gift Mixes

Often you will find that people have more than one gift. That is also true of ascension gifts, however it is unlikely that you will see someone operate in all of them, except Jesus of course. These are people that may have strong **gift** mixes or even **calling** mixes. For example, one may be an apostle and a prophet, or a prophet and teacher. It is not, at all, uncommon to see a pastor that also teaches, however all pastors are not **ascension gift** teachers. Moreover, you may find an ascension gift evangelist that is also an ascension gift prophet. You may see that someone is an ascension gift prophet but at times will simply evangelize. Or, an ascension gift teacher that flows in the gift of prophecy at times. This is because they may have a **calling** but operate in other anointings or gifts.

Commonly, an apostle may flow in many gifts. Apostles are a kind of Kingdom wild card. We see that with Paul. He was definitely an apostle but because apostles have the charge to raise up and send others, they may sometimes operate in greater measure. For example, you may see an apostle that has strong teaching, evangelistic, prophetic and pastoral gifts or any combination of several. However, this doesn't mean that they occupy all five callings simultaneously.

Some modern-day examples of calling mixes are Jennifer LeClaire, who is both an apostle and prophet. John Paul Jackson was briefly a pastor earlier in his ministry, but he was also a prophet and a teacher. Kris Vallotton of Bethel Church in Redding, California is a prophet and pastor. Chuck Pierce is an apostle, prophet and teacher. Though you may see one title associated with their name, you can study the **fruit of their ministry** which shows much more.

It also is worth mentioning that the *old wineskin* (or way of doing things in the kingdom) dictated that the highest order of leadership in a church be that of a pastor. We know that the Word does not state that, so reformation in our church structures are urgently needed to build the Kingdom here on earth *as God intended*. This is why you may see some in leadership shift from pastor to an apostle or prophet, etc. – because these **callings** were, and in some cases still are, ignored. This may possibly be why some begin as pastors *(this does not apply to everyone of course)*. Although, some may *not* have been a pastor at all. It may just be that they had a pronounced calling on their lives, and it was mistaken for pastoring because that was/is the only type of top leadership expression available.

April Moore

Furthermore, it is important to note that no matter what title one in leadership is given, God had a plan for every life **from the beginning.** When the Bible refers to us having been shaped in the womb, it means we were born being who we are, even if our surroundings can't fully comprehend a lane for us. One does not simply **decide** to be an ascension gift officer; it is **revealed** by God when the timing is ripe for what He put in you to expand to a higher influence. What you were born to do should not be frustrating, season in and season out. If it's your grace, yes there will be fiery trials, but there should be a level of ease in **being** who you were born to be (rather than filling some spot for performance). **Fruit will always be evident of the nature of your call, and whether it is that of the offices or not.**

The Process

All gifts require some form of process, usually starting with character. We should never seek to be used by God without also asking Him to **make us ready** to accommodate the tasks, giftings, callings and assignments before us. The core of who we are and how we relate to the world around us fashions us to embody the calling. It is like saying you are hardwired for the calling and you **become the gift** to others. If God calls you to ascension gift ministry in one or more areas, He anoints you for it even if it is not activated right away.

This is just how it was with David when he was anointed King in 1 Samuel 16. He was not activated into his anointed office of King of Judah until 2 Samuel 2 – after many battles, relationship conflicts and quite a bit of running. We have heard that patience is a virtue. Daniel was a great example of one that kept himself in a place of **humility** and allowed God to use him for whatever purpose, in whatever time, that God chose. And, he received even more territory when he became King over all of Israel in 2 Samuel 5.

Daniel was a prophet, but he was only in positions of influence during the reign of certain Kings. Otherwise, we don't hear anything else from him. Could he have been operating under his anointing in other ways? Yes. It just may not be recorded in the Bible. This shows us that process, waiting, and gift and character development is needed because it births maturity in us. And, if we are not walking in some level of **maturity**, how will we help others to mature? Many feel they are an **ascension gift** as soon as they are called. But this is error because some are ready but many are not when they are called. You *must* be processed in maturity for the call so that you can help others reach maturity. You can operate in **gifts of the Holy Spirit** at any stage, and your **design gifts** mature as you naturally mature. But God must process and fashion your life through a series of saying yes to Him and layers of crushing so that you can be poured out as mature wine. For some, they are in the process long before they hear the call. But that is not everyone's experience.

April Moore

Another Look at Service (Diakonia)

We saw this word earlier and stated that it is translated either **service** or **ministry**. There are two applications for it: we saw it as a gift before and now we see it as an **act of our will** as it relates to callings. The bottom line is ministry means service. Instead, we have, at times, seen people in the body of Christ reach levels of ministry and desire to *be* served; it is the other way around. The **ministry** aspect of service is indicated when referring to an office of ministry such as: *bishop, deacon, elder, evangelist, apostle, prophet, teacher,* etc. However, the **service *(diakonia)*** definition refers to **meeting needs** literally through charitable acts or food preparation. So how does the service of a bishop compare to one who serves food? Of course, the functions are different, but both show humility and how important the people of God are. It takes a **heart of servitude** when ministering to the people of God. That is the major connection. Neither an usher nor prophet is more important in the Kingdom, but the realm of **influence** may be different, the level of **sacrifice** may be different, and the **work** may be different. Jesus explained it best in Matthew 20:22-28. The mother of Zebedee's sons came to Jesus with her sons. She asked Him to allow her two sons to sit on Jesus' right hand and the other on the left, in His kingdom. Starting at verse 22, Jesus answered and said, "You do not know what you ask. Are you able to drink the cup that I am about to drink, and be baptized with the baptism that I am baptized with?" They said to Him, "We are able." Here is Jesus's response:

So, He said to them, "You will indeed drink My cup, and be baptized with the baptism that I am baptized with; but to sit on My right hand and on My left is not Mine to give, but it is for those for whom it is prepared by My Father." And when the ten heard it, they were greatly displeased with the two brothers. But Jesus called them to Himself and said, "You know that the rulers of the Gentiles lord it over them, and those who are great exercise authority over them. <u>Yet it shall not be so among you; but whoever desires to become great among you, let him be your servant. And whoever desires to be first among you, let him be your slave— just as the Son of Man did not come to be served, but to serve, and to give His life a ransom for many."</u> (Matt 20:23-28)

We are all called to be ministers in one form or another, but I will mostly address this to those with ascension gifts. As you minister, you should freely operate in your realm of calling. *Please remember this as you read the rest of this paragraph.* Know that your life is not your own, you were bought with a price, and as you minister in any capacity you said yes to God. Whether you are even a deacon or an apostle, you said yes to God and agreed to minister to His people. The carnal eye sees only the glory in ministry, but the glory is there to help serve and to fulfil whatever needs people have. It is not meant for us to get "drunk" off the glory we operate in by allowing our egos to be consumed with the gifts and callings on our lives. We pour out to **serve** those who need it. Many times, power to minister is there in spite of trials that we deal with personally. This is because we were processed, matured, and can handle more. We are chosen to reach a greater multitude of people on the platform God gave us. That makes us a mature servant of many. We labor and seek after God to find out where the need is, God gives us the answer, and we deliver it. It is a beautiful thing. So, if Jesus could wash feet why can't we who minister be willing to *really* touch the lives of people? As referenced in Mark 10:45, "Just as the Son of Man did not come to

April Moore

be served, but *to* serve, and to give His life a ransom for many," are you willing to drink the cup that is required for your calling?

Remember, when we are called to an ascension gift, we **become** the gift. God takes our life and molds us in greater measure. He purifies and fashions us so that He can use us in greater capacity.

There are major differences in the gifts of the Holy Spirit, the design gifts, and having a calling. I say this because teaching and prophecy show up in both areas. Sometimes people are confused between a prophet and one who prophesies. There is also misunderstanding between the **teaching gift** and the **teacher calling**. Likewise, the **apostle** gifting is sometimes confused with **administration** or **leadership**. **Evangelists** can be misconstrued for the **exhortation gift,** and the **leadership gifting** with the **pastor calling**. This will often happen when operating in the callings mentioned. We need to make a clear distinction between the different giftings to eliminate misunderstanding. Some may be asking why making that distinction is important. After all, we can just be led by God, we can just flow and operate in giftings – it doesn't matter what you call it. If that is your question, I understand your thought process. However, every gift, be it natural or spiritual, has a development process. You don't become a master in any craft, or in this case gifting, if you are unaware of what it is and how it operates. These gifts are powerful weapons in the hands of those that are skilled in them and highly effective in sharpening others. You would never operate a high capacity weapon without training. The gifts supersede leveling the playing field against the kingdom of darkness!

If you connect with your giftings and activate them, you will be a force to be reckoned with in the spirit realm.

Ascension Gifts

Now that we have a good background on these gifts, we will now look at what they are. It is important to understand that the foundation of churches and ministries should model the foundation that **Christ** spoke to us through Paul. In 1 Corinthians 12:27-28, it is stated that, "Now you are the body of Christ, and members individually. **And God has appointed these in the church: first apostles, second prophets, third teachers**, after that miracles, then gifts of healings, helps, administrations, varieties of tongues." So, we will take a look at these three **foundational callings** and move on to the pastor and evangelist. This is important because many churches are missing the relevance and significance of these callings. The world is speeding by, but the church is needs to be effective in catching up to advance the Kingdom! Ideally, church leadership should reflect **all ascension gifts** which means, in some cases, de-centralizing the pastor (which we will later discuss). God gave us the blueprint, so we ought to embrace it.

April Moore

Apostles

Apostolos (ap-os'-tol-os)- Most commonly defined as a "sent one" or messenger that has been given a charge or instruction.

God sends these people to build the foundation of new ministries and churches. They are also **reformers** of existing structures that need change and progress. They are the **first layer** of the foundation mentioned in 1 Corinthians 12:28 so they are *sent* to establish. They establish order and send others out as a release. Mature apostles do not hoard gifted people within the four walls of their churches and ministries; they see to it that people are sent in various ways to continue advancing the Kingdom. Apostles can be **overseers** of other churches that are led by apostles or pastors. They also carry an authority about them as they head and oversee people and ministries in the Kingdom. Some apostles are over Apostolic Centers and Kingdom Centers *(like Kingdom Enlightenment Ministries)* that specialize in equipping, establishing, and sending out leaders.

You will see that some apostles have a strong gift of **administration**. However, they move in and out of many gifts, similarly to the life of Paul. At times, they will function under different callings as well. Because they help to establish the foundation of churches and ministries, they need to identify with various gifts and callings. This is so that they can see gifts in others and know what is needed to prepare people to walk in their gifts. **But this is not a rule.**

Many Apostles are strong visionaries that see the broad picture. They often do not want to be entangled in small details. Because of this, if they do not have strong interpersonal skills, people that serve with them may feel looked over. It is not that they don't love people. They do what they do **because** of God's people. It is just that they have a mandate to thrust everyone higher. In order to maintain focus and steer the ship, they must stay alert and involved in the bigness of the vision. A true Apostle will provoke you to growth and will not stay in a vein that pacifies or nurses your wounds. So, depending on gift/ calling mix, they may not always come across as a nurturer the way most view nurturers. In contrast, Pastors are among the best nurturers, they are the ones to go to for that type of healing. Apostles will charge you with a plan to dust off, get healing, and keep moving because the Kingdom needs you in position!

Calling Attributes
- Likes to **start** new ministries or churches, set them up and **delegate** others to run the ministry
- Wants to **raise** up others that are gifted and **release** them into their field of ministry
- Able to minister to people from **various backgrounds and cultures**

April Moore

- Leaders and pastors often come to this person for **direction, shifting, advancement,** and **insight**

Apostles in Scripture

- Acts 14:4 (Paul and Barnabas)
- Acts 1 (Matthias)
- Philippians 2:25 (Epaphroditus)
- Romans 16:7 (Andronicus and Junia, a female apostle)
- Matthew 10:2-4 (The 12 disciples of Christ, who were also referred to as apostles)
- I Thessalonians 1:1 and 2:6 (Timothy and Silvanus)
- Galatians 1:19 (James, the brother of Jesus)
- Hebrews 3:1 (Jesus, the "Apostle and High Priest of our profession")

Modern-Day Apostles

- Becky Castle of Launch Houston
- Ryan LeStrange
- Chuck Pierce
- Dutch Sheets
- John Eckhardt

- Jenifer LeClaire
- Bill Johnson
- C. Peter Wagner
- Bill Hamon

Prophets

Prophetes (prof-ay'-tace)- A foreteller who is inspired to speak. Prophets are also referred to as one who interprets the oracles of God and explains His deep mysteries.

Prophet is the second ascension gift, listed in 1 Corinthians 12:28, to establish the foundation of the church. This is another vital ministry largely missing in most local church bodies. In short, a prophet is God's **mouthpiece** in the body of Christ, relaying the mind of God as their function. This is someone that has insight into the blueprint God has set forth for seasons and moves of God. Prophets give a Word from the Lord with more authority than you would see operating in the *gift* of prophecy. A prophet will foretell events before they happen, as well as **communicate** the purposes, plans, will, and corrections of the Lord. It is important to note that God *also* reveals His **redemptive plan** *after* correction through the prophets. To be that in-tuned with God takes intimacy and a worship-filled lifestyle.

Shamar (shaw-mar)- to keep, watch, preserve.

April Moore

Prophets also have **protective functions** to the body of Christ as intercessors. Not every intercessor is a prophet, but every prophet's role requires intercession. How that looks may vary from prophet to prophet. This is because they can serve as a communication mediator between God and man. They see things coming from afar and are able to intercede and combat it before it happens. Habakkuk 2:1 explains this as Habakkuk sets himself as a **watchman** for this very reason. Also, in the book *The Shamar Prophet* by John Eckhardt, he highlights in 2 Kings 13:20 that while Elisha was alive, the land was **safe** because of the protective power of a prophet. Elisha's death is mentioned, and in the very next sentence, it is tied to the Moabite invasion. This means the **governmental authority** of prophets can cover lands. Oh, that the prophets would arise and defend the land with authority and intercession!

And Elisha died, and they buried him. And the bands of the Moabites invaded the land at the coming in of the year.

Likewise, in Samuel's time, this was evident as well.

So, the Philistines were subdued, and they did not come anymore within the border of Israel. And the hand of the Lord was against the Philistines all the days of Samuel. (1 Samuel 7:3 NASB)

Also, Elisha did not only intercede, he also knew the **secrets of God's heart** and was able to hear the **strategy** of the opposing king trying to ambush Israel. It happened several times to where the king of Aram thought he had a mole leaking information to Israel. But there was a Prophet in Israel that could hear from Heaven and speak to kings!

> *Now the heart of the king of Aram was enraged over this thing; and he called his servants and said to them, "Will you tell me which of us is for the king of Israel?" One of his servants said, "No, my lord, O king; but Elisha, the prophet who is in Israel, tells the king of Israel the words that you speak in your bedroom." (2 Kings 6:11-12 NASB)*

It is said that the gift of intercession is not listed in the Bible. This is true. Although, while observing even non-prophets that have a deep intercessory burden, it *does* appear to be a calling – but not an ascension gift calling. Remember from earlier in this chapter, there are thousands and even millions of callings both inside and outside of a Christian setting.

One thing to note regarding prophets is that it is a **peculiar walk**. Often, prophets have a history of rejection because they seem to be wired differently than others. This is because they are trained to deal with the **unseen realm** and may not even be released to share what they see, hear, or sense with others. Which is also why it is important for them to intercede – they will see things they cannot deal with in the natural. Ezekiel stands out as one who truly understood what this meant.

> *Then I looked, and there was a likeness, like the appearance of fire—from the appearance of His waist and downward, fire; and from His waist and upward, like the appearance of brightness, like the color of amber. He stretched out the form of a hand and took me by a lock of my hair; and the Spirit lifted me up between earth and heaven, and brought me in visions of God to Jerusalem, to the door of the north gate of the inner court, where the seat of the image of jealousy was, which provokes to jealousy. And behold, the glory of the God of Israel was there, like the vision that I saw in the plain. Then He said to me, "Son of man, lift your eyes now toward the north." So, I lifted my eyes toward the north, and there, north of the altar gate, was this image of*

April Moore

jealousy in the entrance. Furthermore, He said to me, "Son of man, do you see what they are doing, the great abominations that the house of Israel commits here, to make Me go far away from My sanctuary? Now turn again, you will see greater abominations." So, He brought me to the door of the court; and when I looked, there was a hole in the wall. Then He said to me, "Son of man, dig into the wall"; and when I dug into the wall, there was a door. And, while still seeing in the spirit, Ezekiel witnessed God judging these people for their actions, and in the spirit realm raised up warrior angels that presided over that region to bring death to these people who sinned against God. (Ezekiel 8:3-8)

Here is another experience Ezekiel had in the spirit realm. It is relevant because it shows how prophets bear witness to supernatural happenings, behind the scenes of the natural realm.

*Then He called out **in my hearing** with a loud voice, saying, 'Let those who have charge over the city draw near, each with a deadly weapon in his hand.' And suddenly six men came from the direction of the upper gate, which faces north, each with his battle-ax in his hand. One man among them was clothed with linen and had a writer's inkhorn at his side. They went in and stood beside the bronze altar. Now the glory of the God of Israel had gone up from the cherub, where it had been, to the threshold of the temple. And He called to the man clothed with linen, who had the writer's inkhorn at his side; and the Lord said to him, 'Go through the midst of the city, through the midst of Jerusalem, and put a mark on the foreheads of the men who sigh and cry over all the abominations that are done within it.' To the others He said **in my hearing**, 'Go after him through the city and kill; do not let your eye spare, nor have any pity.' (Ezekiel 9:1-5)*

In verse 8, Ezekiel responded with **prayer**, by pleading with God. It states:

"So it was, that while they were killing them, I was left alone; and I fell on my face and cried out, and said, "Ah, Lord God! Will You destroy all the remnant of Israel in pouring out Your fury on Jerusalem?"

Thankfully, **all** judgment has been poured out at the cross; God is in to **redeeming** mankind and the earth. Therefore, all the experiences and messages that prophets have should reflect this **reconciling** quality of God.

The term "Old Testament prophet" is often used of those prophets that lack mercy. They lean toward judgement. However, I disagree with that term and view it as a lack of understanding about the heart perspective God wants them to have. Even many Old Testament Prophets prayed for mercy on behalf of God's people. Prophets such as Moses who prayed for God to stop destroying the disobedient. Abraham asked if God would destroy Sodom and Gomorrah if there were any righteous inhabitants. And Jeremiah wept over the people and desired to see them turn back to God. And God responded to their intercession of mercy. Be warry of those who take joy, or are swift to proclaim judgement never having explored the redemptive heart of God toward the people.

Another difficulty for a prophet is patience, but different than the Teacher as you will read later. Many times, prophets see what is coming before others perceive it. One of their charges is to prepare people for moves of God and potential bumps in the road. When people have difficulty seeing or heeding prophetic words, prophets can get a bit antsy. Know that the authority in a prophet, through prayer, can potentially shift the road ahead if they remain in prayer with their ear to God's mouth. God is indeed sovereign, though waiting for others to catch up to their understanding can be uncomfortable for a prophet.

Calling Attributes

- Delivers personal and corporate messages to the body for **edification, rebuke, warning,** and **guidance**.

April Moore

- Responsible for guiding the corporate body of Christ toward the plans and moves of God or away from things that God is warning about.
- Is given redemptive insight on how to confront someone so they will line back up with God's plan for their lives.
- Lead people into deeper spiritual insight behind circumstances.
- From the seat of **love** and **mercy**, they are called to intercede for people, congregations, regions and/or nations.
- Prophets must stand strong on the Word of God regardless of how the recipient receives it.
- Also, see "Prophecy" as a gifting in an earlier chapter.

Prophets in Scripture

- Moses
- Isaiah 8:3 (Isaiah and his wife, a prophetess)
- Jeremiah
- Luke 2:36 (Anna)
- Judges 4 (Deborah, prophetess, wife and a judge over Israel)
- Phillip was an Evangelist, but his four virgin daughters were Prophetesses seen in Acts 21:8-9
- Acts 21:10-11 (Agabus)

- Matthew 11:9-11 (John the Baptist)
- Jesus

Modern-Day Prophets

- John Paul Jackson
- James Goll
- Kris Vallotton
- Graham Cooke
- Jennifer LeClaire
- Kim Clement

Teachers

Didaskalos (did-as'-kal-os)- instructor, master, to be competent in theology.

The teacher is the third ascension gift that is listed in building the foundation of ministry. Teacher means instructor and, as a calling, one would say a **master in instruction**. They have the ability to systematically instruct believers through their development and training. Not only are they able to instruct from the Word of God, but they can find **what is needed** to instruct. Teachers are very **resourceful** in that way. They are skilled in **accessing the education gaps** in their community and can implement training resources to fill those needs. They also teach us **how to live** as people of God. The frameworks of our minds are **shaped** by teachers in one form or another, which means the decisions we make can be the results of the teaching we've received. How much more so is the importance of a teacher *in the Body of Christ*? Think about it! Teachers impart Biblical principles to parents, who in turn teach their children, who are rising up to make an impact on the world. The calling of a teacher affects many generations after them! Teaching can **change culture** and **break demonic systems over the minds of people**.

Unfortunately, teachers are not always seen as being the powerful Kingdom assets they are. This is largely due to flaws in some church structures, which are not built Biblically according to 1 Corinthians 12:27-28. Jesus, *as a prophet,* told us the mind of God, but *as a teacher,* He explained to us **how** to live according to the plan God was establishing for us. This began the shift for believers, and it is still affecting us to this very day.

One area of pitfall that teachers must take caution in is arrogance. They have an uncanny ability to gather and distribute information. Without a true heart of love toward the body of Christ, teachers may be condescending toward those who have a hard time understanding things. This is why maturity is so important. A teacher may feel light years ahead of others in their understanding but must patiently wait for others to catch up. Indeed, it is their job to assist others in this.

Calling Attributes

- Is masterful in **communicating** the Bible
- Motivates and influences **the way people think** through the Word of God
- Gets agitated when scripture is used incorrectly
- A **researcher** of Biblical truths in order to explain it to others
- Intuitively lead by the Spirit on **how** to explains things to people.

Teachers in Scripture

- Paul who wrote 2/3 of the New Testament
- Acts 18:24-25 (Apollos)
- Mark 9:5 (Jesus was referred to as Rabbi which means Teacher. He was constantly found teaching.)

Modern-Day Teachers

- John Paul Jackson
- Andrew Wommack
- Beth Moore
- Joyce Meyer

April Moore

- Marilyn Hickey

Pastors

Poimen (poy-mane')- shepherd.

Many analogies over time have been made regarding the pastor and a shepherd. A shepherd **cares for the well-being of the flock**. Jesus said in John 10:27, "My sheep hear My voice, and I know them, and they follow Me." The pastor is a very **relational** role, more so than the other ascension gifts, because it requires devoted and dedicated commitment to the people of God. While ministering, the prophet would intuitively approach from a spiritual perspective and apply it to the natural. However, the pastor will see the **practical issues** and **encourage spiritual growth** from that standpoint. So, how one ministers to produce spiritual growth is relative to the perspective of their mantle. Pastors are great for **discipleship**; they enjoy watching others grow and overcome obstacles. This type of **dedication** requires helping the people of God through the trials of life, including crises and emotional, relational or life changes. We haven't discussed fruit throughout the gifts, but the pastor requires **longsuffering**. They need it for those that may seem to hear the advice given, yet continue not applying the knowledge or falling due to strongholds. Pastors are big **givers**, full of **compassion**, but will sometimes need to create boundaries (not walls) to guard their hearts.

One of the areas of church today that is in process of reformation is the centralization of the pastor. Many churches are very pastor-centered, which is a model that completely ignores what Jesus wanted to establish. Unlike the apostle, the pastor **nurtures** and may have a hard time delegating. Apostles are gifted in raising people up to run in their anointing. The pastor keeps the sheep close – nurtures and cares for the sheep. This mentality does not foster expanded growth in most people. Instead, it fosters dependence if it is not balanced with other ascension ministry gifts in the headship. Because of this, the pastor should have apostolic oversight to bring order to their ministries.

Pastors are not Biblically, nor metaphorically, married to the congregation! If so, it would be adulterous, because the Bride (the congregation, *including* the pastor) belongs to Christ. There is a tendency in pastors to labor beyond the measures of their time and energy, thus sometimes causing their families or marriages to be neglected. Natural responsibilities and commitments were not meant to be in jeopardy in the lives of pastors because of their over-involvement with church members day and night. If you will allow the sheep to grow, not just so that they will be better spiritually, but so that they mature, some may take on higher roles within the ministry (and therefore, be a relief to leadership). Every call and counseling session should not be allocated to the senior pastor. There should be other pastors raised up to help carry the load. This also means that

April Moore

everyone that is raised up as a pastor, does not necessarily need to head their own church.

Regarding pastoral responsibility, we have been taught the opposite for so many generations. Nevertheless, don't take my word for it; consider Moses. He escaped to Midian and became a shepherd. He kept that staff when he went back to deliver Israel from the hands of Pharaoh, but he kept the shepherd mentality even after he left. He needed Jethro to look with **apostolic eyes** and say that he needed to de-centralize his dealings with the flock. He let him know that he was tiring himself out, as well as the people. Think about it, his "congregation" was very large, and it is impossible for **one man** to lead such a large group of people, single-handedly. There were 603,550 men that left Egypt under Moses' leadership, which would mean that there were about 2 to 2.5 million people that he shepherded. And, they *all* wanted to come to him for help, to settle disputes, to complain about their hungry bellies, etc. Here is the discourse between Moses and his Father-in-law, Jethro:

> *And so, it was, on the next day, that Moses sat to judge the people; and the people stood before Moses **from morning until evening**. So when Moses' father-in-law saw all that he did for the people, he said, "What is this thing that you are doing for the people? Why do you **alone** sit, and all the people stand before you from morning until evening?" And Moses said to his father-in-law, "Because the people come to me to inquire of God. When they have a difficulty, they come to me, and I judge between one and another; and I make known the statutes of God and His laws." So Moses' father-in-law said to him, "The thing that you do is not good. Both you and these people who are with you will surely **wear yourselves out**. For this thing is **too much for you**; you are not able to perform it **by yourself**. Listen now to my voice; I will give you counsel, and God will be with you: Stand before God for the people, so that you may bring the difficulties to God. And you shall teach them the statutes and the laws, and show them the way in which they must walk and the work they must do. Moreover, you shall select from all the people able men, such as fear God, men of truth, hating covetousness; and place such over them to be rulers of thousands, rulers of hundreds,*

rulers of fifties, and rulers of tens. And let them judge the people at all times. Then it will be that **every great matter they shall bring to you, but every small matter they themselves shall judge. So, it will be easier for you, for they will bear the burden with you.** *If you do this thing, and God so commands you, then you will be able to endure, and all this people will also go to their place in peace." So, Moses heeded the voice of his father-in-law and did all that he had said. (Exodus 18:13-24)*

It only took Jethro one day to see that what Moses was doing was not a sustainable model of leadership. Left to himself, Moses may not have recognized what he was doing was a real issue. And if he did see that his system was flawed, he may not have been able to figure out how to solve it because he was not gifted in that area to have that perspective. Make no mistake, Moses was an excellent leader; it is just that Moses was wired to shepherd and hear from God to help the people. Note that although Moses saw God face to face, this advice came through a trusted advisor instead of God directly.

Moses had a family but, with the burden of 2 million people solely on his shoulders, I can imagine the marital neglect and how difficult it would have been to truly be there and present for his children. God blessed us with families and anointing but **balance** is our choice. The anointing is always there and will produce results when pulled on. Remember that Jesus did not have to consciously heal the woman with the issue of blood; she pulled directly on His anointing and got results (Luke 8:43-48). This is something to lookout for because if one does not manage it, a seemingly great thing can open the door for destruction in other areas. **Delegate and live**!

April Moore

Calling Attributes

- Concerned about the spiritual and emotional **well-being of others**
- Enjoys discipling others and "**walking them through**" life's challenges
- Will desire to check on those that may have fallen away to **pull them back in**.
- Will assist people in returning to God – those that have backslidden
- Has a **huge heart for people** and wants to see people grow in God
- Feel they have the heart of a shepherd to care for others and help show them the ways of God

Pastors in Scripture

- Titus and Timothy- Though they may have walked in other offices as well, they were trained as pastors through their respective epistles (the books Titus and Timothy). These books are also known as the Pastoral Epistles.
- Romans 16:3-5 (Aquila and Priscilla, husband & wife co-pastors) They show up in several places, but it is most prominent that they had meetings and discipled in their home.
- John 10:27 (Jesus)

Modern-Day Pastors

- John Hagee
- Charles Stanley
- Charles Swindoll
- Brian and Bobbie Houston
- Ed Young
- Ron Carpenter
- Kirbyjon Caldwell

Evangelists

Euaggelistes (yoo-ang-ghel-is-tace')- one who preaches the gospel of Jesus Christ.

The gospel means good tidings. The refreshing good news that Jesus came to save the lost and restore His Kingdom is vital to advancement and growth in the Kingdom of God. An evangelist is one that is **driven to lead others to Christ**. Their **passion for winning souls** can consume them at times. They think of ways to **draw people** in order to effectively minister to them. These people can get across the gospel in ways that others may find difficult, but because they are anointed to reach the lost, they will get responses. Effective evangelists **capitalize on love and the use of spiritual gifts** to show the **power** of God to draw people to Christ.

Acts 21:8 mentions that Philip was an evangelist and he was also one of the first deacons. Also, earlier in Acts 8, we learn of some exciting events with Philip. After scattering due to persecution from

Saul in Jerusalem, Philip went to Samaria and enthusiastically **preached to them**. Those in Samaria were those in whom Jews normally saw little value, but Philip **saw their value**. Evangelists can have a natural pull for those that have been rejected, forgotten or are otherwise disadvantaged. In Acts 8, it says that he preached about Christ and **healed many** and **cast out unclean spirits** in Samaria. When the group decided to start traveling back to Jerusalem, the Lord had different travel plans for Philip. An angel of the Lord came to Philip and told him to go to a desert road that descended from Jerusalem to Gaza. Acts 8:27-31 states:

> *So, he arose and went. And behold, a man of Ethiopia, a eunuch of great authority under Candace the queen of the Ethiopians, who had charge of all her treasury, and had come to Jerusalem to worship, was returning. And sitting in his chariot, he was reading Isaiah the prophet. Then the Spirit said to Philip, "Go near and overtake this chariot." So Philip ran to him, and heard him reading the prophet Isaiah, and said, "Do you understand what you are reading?" And he said, "How can I, unless someone **guides** me?" And he asked Philip to come up and sit with him.*

Philip began to preach all about Jesus and explain the scriptures, to where the eunuch was ready to receive Jesus as his Lord and Savior.

> *Now as they went down the road, they came to some water. And the eunuch said, "See, here is water. What hinders me from being **baptized**?" Then Philip said, "If you believe with all your heart, you may." And he answered and said, "I believe that Jesus Christ is the Son of God." So, he commanded the chariot to stand still. And both Philip and the eunuch went down into the water, and **he baptized him**. Now when they came up out of the water, the Spirit of the Lord caught Philip away, so that the eunuch saw him no more; and he went on his way rejoicing. But Philip was found at Azotus. And passing through, he preached in all the cities till he came to Caesarea. (Acts 8:36-40)*

We see the **supernatural** activated in the ministry of Philip – from healings, casting out demons and even **supernatural travel**

arrangements where the Spirit caught Philip away and placed him in a different area. Because of what we see in the Word of God, we can believe that God can do **absolutely anything** through us in ministry while serving His people and winning people to Christ.

Many evangelists are acquainted with the darkness of society. In their maturation process they must be keen on the balance between walking in the Holiness of God while still being relatable. A lot of evangelists were pulled out of very dark places prior to receiving Christ. This is true for many of us, but their fire for winning the lost typically shows up quickly after salvation. They start running and recruiting right away! They would do well to have people in their lives they are accountable to so that they take care not to blend in with the issues of those in which they are actually called to minister. If not, they can gravitate toward darkness and get consumed there, instead of being more of a Fire Fighter where they are to run in and pull people out to safety. Again, maturity is everything! And I will explain soon **an important key for every ascension gift**.

Evangelists also often have a hard time staying in one place because they are built for movement. Going out and finding the lost drives them. Of course, the gift and calling mix of the Evangelist can prove to be different from one to another. But in general, when training evangelists, you must keep them moving and activating while balancing that movement with training time.

April Moore

Calling Attributes

- Able to explain the gospel clearly with **power to draw** the hearer
- Can feel the heaviness of the pull to **go and reach** the lost
- Some have a strong pull that time is running out and they must **win souls** as much as possible
- Finds themselves **speaking to strangers** and eventually turning the conversation toward Christ
- Will study the Word to become **well versed** on rebuttals to overcome objection to the gospel
- Typically, will **share their testimony** of how Christ saved them and the wonderful transformation that it brought to their lives

Evangelists in Scripture

- Matthew, Mark, Luke and John were considered evangelists because of their account of the 4 gospels. Each of them gave a clear account of the good news of Jesus Christ and it has been winning souls ever since.
- The Woman at the Well, John 4:39-42
- Philip, Acts 21:8
- Jesus, because every word He spoke was the gospel and pointed us to His salvation for us

Modern-Day Evangelists

- Billy Graham, Franklin Graham, and Will Graham
- Reinhard Bonnke with Christ for All Nations
- Todd White
- Jesse Duplantis
- Kirk Cameron
- Oral Roberts
- Paul and Jan Crouch
- William Joseph Seymour (started the Pentecostal Movement on Azusa Street)

Ascension Gift Key

One of the absolute most important of all keys regarding ascension gifts is unification. And I don't **only** mean that everyone should be able to get along. I say this because peace among believers is a by-product of unity. The Kingdom of God has been stunted in valuable growth and maturation due to a lack of deposits from all ascension gifts. ***Together* you can operate and govern so much better. Alone, you will build partial works without seeing the manifestation of the fullness of Christ that Ephesians 4 speaks about.**

So, I leave something with you. It is time for all 5 ascension gifts to rise up, work together, and build! Every single one of these gifts is unto the glory of God and the reigning of Christ through His people. So, ascension gifts, I speak to you to govern well and build with each other. Learn how to work together and keep your focus while pointing others to Christ in the way that you are uniquely built!

Journal Questions:

1. What are some of the key things that you learned about ascension gifts?

2. Did you know that ascension gifts were still in operation?

Your Charge

Now that you have been armed with more knowledge and insight in *Gifts and Callings*, I charge you to practice them. Don't sit on them and lose your drive. Seek God to give more clarification on how the gifts flow in you. Also, continue your study. Once you discover your gifts, allow yourself to grow higher than the foundations of the gift. Seek further training and make it your business to start using them. Know that without God you cannot operate or develop in the giftings.

The Holy Spirit is our trainer. If you make yourself available to be used by God in this way, it will open up a whole new dimension to your Christian walk. In addition, remember the key to the giftings is *serving others*. We want the Kingdom of God to manifest here in the earth realm, so allow the gifts to be the tool that does that very thing in your life and the lives of those around you!

April Moore

Prayer of Activation

Father, I thank you for the gifts (or callings) that you entrusted to me. I ask that you **illuminate** and **activate** those you would have me to operate in during this time. Teach me how to use them and allow me to operate in them with integrity, confidence, and grace. I shatter every plot of the enemy that would try to cause me to shrink back in fear or confusion. I speak to my flesh to submit to the guiding of the Holy Spirit and not succumb to error or fear. Lord use me to operate in my gifting wherever You choose. In the Name of Jesus, so be it!

APPENDIX

Appendix - Bishops, Elders and Deacons

Callings were discussed earlier and how the local church body may recognize someone as operating in an ascension gift. If the senior leadership of the church body sees a person is ready to be elevated into office/position, that person may be commissioned or ordained into office. With this in mind, there are a few other offices/positions that are mentioned in the Bible, but they are not designated as gifts or ascension gifts. However, they can be vitally important to a functioning church body. These are that of a bishop, elder, and deacon. They are not ascension gifts so they are positions that one may **desire** to assume. But like those with ascension gifts, it is highly recommended that these positions be occupied by those in leadership who are **mature**, especially bishops and elders, because they bear greater responsibilities for the people. It is worth noting that though you will get the Biblical foundation on these positions here, the local church body, in many ways, has expanded the operation of some of these roles.

Bishops

Episkopos (ep-is'-kop-os)- a superintendent, watchman, or overseer. In some translations, you may see the word overseer used in place of bishop.

This is a **governing** or **ruling** position in which those appointed **oversee** the church. This position also denotes a **pastoral function**. The overseeing aspect of a bishop is not specified in detail so that we know the exact overseeing function, but we do know that the description of a bishop is strikingly similar to that of an elder. Also, bishops, many times, are used synonymously with that of an apostle even though their functions are very different. So, in many modern cases, the role has expanded to be that of one who may oversee many churches. None the less, their role is not only overseeing and governing aspects of one local body.

Scriptures that explain basic qualifications and give further reference/context: Philippians 1:1, 1 Timothy 3:1-7, and Titus 1:7-9 (shows an elder functioning as a bishop and gives qualifications).

Elders

Presbuteros (pres-boo'-ter-os)- one who is a presbyter. A presbyter is one who exercises teaching and administrative functions.

Biblically, this is also a **governing** role and one you most commonly see in the local body as doing such. An elder's governing oversight helps to **make decisions**, **give direction** and is also considered a pastoral type of role in the way they **advise** and **guide** people. An elder is a position of honor and dignity as one who is older either by way of age, experience or wisdom. As an elder, there is power and authority that follows them as a minister as we see in James 5:14. An interesting note is that elders were around since the time of Moses, and they play an active role in the church today just as they did in those times, and even more so. Elders continue to exist and give direction even in the throne room of God (Rev 4:2-4, Rev 4:9-11, Rev 5:5-14)

Scriptures that explain basic qualifications and give further reference or mention in New Testament context: Acts 14:21-23, Acts 15:1-29 (shows a process in which the Apostles and Elders settled a matter), 1 Timothy 4:14, 1 Timothy 5:17-22, James 5:14, 1 Peter 5:1-5 (shepherd function), Titus 1:1-9 (qualifications are blended with Bishops).

Deacons

Diakonos (dee-ak'-on-os)- a servant or minister that serves the practical needs of the people.

This is one of the most misused functions in the church body today. This is because, in some cases, deacons are used to **govern**, but that is not the Biblical reason they were installed. The elders and bishops have that governing function. Nonetheless, deacons are extremely important in the Body of Christ. Their function was created to do what the ascension gifts or the elders could not do – to **meet the needs of people in ways the others could not**, because of their weighty responsibilities. This means that if deacons are not in place, there are areas of ministry that fall to the ground.

So, what does a Deacon do? In the Word of God, deacons worked alongside ascension gifts, bishops, and elders as a **support role**. Some were even gifted to teach and evangelize like Stephen and Philip. But, primarily, the word for deacon comes from that of **one who serves tables**. They were to **care for practical needs and to help widows**, etc., as seen in Acts 6:1-6. We also see a woman in that role, a deaconess. Her name was Phoebe and we find her in Romans 16:12. Some translations call her a servant which, in the Greek, is the same word used for deacon.

There is one more note regarding deacons. The role of a deacon has been abused in that many have gone against what would qualify one for such a position. So, when some hear the title of deacon, they might have a negative view of the office. I believe that God wants to restore the honor of the deacon position. Please see the scriptures below, but please note 1 Timothy 3:8-13, particularly verse 13: "For those who have served well as deacons obtain for themselves a good standing and great boldness in the faith which is in Christ Jesus."

Scriptures that explain basic qualifications and give further reference/mention in context are: Philippians 1:1, 1 Timothy 3:8-13 (qualifications of a male and female, or deaconess, are described here).

April Moore

Suggested Reading

- *Shamar Prophet by Apostle John Eckhardt (Contact Crusaders Ministries)*
- *The Seer by Jim W. Goll*
- *The School of the Seers by Jonathan Welton*
- *Faith and Confessions by Charles Capps*
- *Basic Training for Prophetic Activation by Dan McCollam*
- *Apostles Prophets and the Coming Moves of God by Dr. Bill Hamon*
- *Understanding 5Fold Ministry by Dr. Stefan Sos*

Dream Interpretation Reference Books

- *The Prophet's Dictionary by Paula A. Price, PH.D*
- *The Divinity Code by Adam F. Thompson & Adrian Beale*

References Used

The Complete Word Study New Testament, © 1991 By AMG International, Inc. Second Edition 1992

The Complete Word Study Dictionary: New Testament, © 1992 By AMG International, Inc. Revised Edition 1993

Thayer's and Smith's Bible Dictionary from The New American Standard New Testament Greek Lexicon

Dictionary.com

Webster.com

ABOUT THE AUTHOR

April Moore, and her husband Morris Moore, are founders of Kingdom Enlightenment Ministries, in which they are faithful commissioned ministers of the Gospel. April has been teaching the Word of God with anointing, revelation and enthusiasm for over 20 years. She dedicates herself to training ministers and leaders by creating and implementing training strategies.

Morris and April Moore are available to train your leaders on Gifts and Callings, as well as many other areas.
Contact KEMinistries@Gmail.com for speaking engagements, seminars and workshops.

Visit Kingdom Enlightenment Ministries, the online store, blog/vlog and more. Also, enter your email to be notified about the upcoming books, trainings and specials.

Scan the QR code or visit http://www.KEMinistries.com

Anointing Oils

Candles

Anointing Oil Scented Wax Melts

Bath & Spa Duo

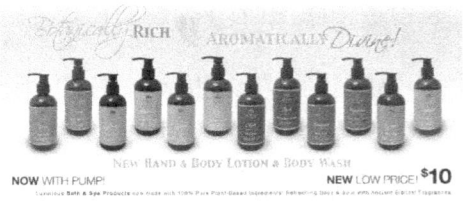

Tallit Prayer Shawls

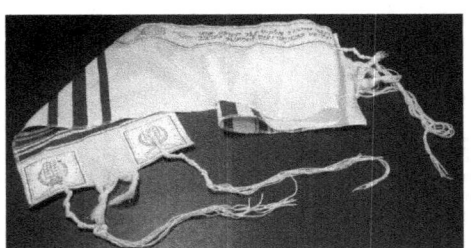

Specialty Anointing Oils

NOTES

www.ingramcontent.com/pod-product-compliance
Lightning Source LLC
Chambersburg PA
CBHW060500010526
44118CB00018B/2478

9780999848264